CHET PRYOR
ENGLISH DEPARTMENT
MONTGOMERY COLLEGE-GERMANTOWN
20200 OBSERVATION DRIVE
GERMANTOWN, MD 20876

Y0-CUL-568

writing: plans, drafts, and revisions

**JOHN HERUM and
D. W. CUMMINGS**
Central Washington State College

RANDOM HOUSE
NEW YORK

writing: plans, drafts, and revisions

Copyright © 1971 by Random House, Inc.

All rights reserved under International and Pan-American Copyright Conventions. Published in the United States by Random House, Inc., New York, and simultaneously in Canada by Random House of Canada Limited, Toronto.

Library of Congress Catalog Card Number: 70–120147

Manufactured in the United States of America. Composed by H. Wolff Book Mfg. Co. Inc. New York, N.Y. Printed and bound by Halliday Lithograph, Corp., West Hanover, Mass.

Standard Book Number: 394–30330–X

Design by J. M. Wall

First Edition
9 8 7 6 5 4 3 2 1

To **JACKIE** and **CAROL**

preface

Part of the craft of a good writer is to make his work seem natural and easy. The better the writer is, the easier his job seems to be. The finished, smooth surface of good prose can create the illusion that the author sat and thought hard until an essay popped out of his forehead, neatly printed, with margins clean and words impeccably in place. The illusion of ease and naturalness is a proper and legitimate goal for a writer. But writing is mostly hard, stubborn work that takes more time and thought than we usually want to give. Accordingly, a good part of the emphasis in *Writing: Plans, Drafts, and Revisions* is on a "backstage look" at writing, where the grub work, the scaffolding, and the debris are hidden.

Drafting is a private act of expression. Editing —or revising—takes what is done in private and makes it ready for a public. This book describes how the privacy of drafting can stimulate and encourage the flow of ideas. It then describes ways to control the mind's sometimes unruly output and ways to edit rough prose so that the thought it embodies is given a clear and public form.

The chapters of this book follow a more or less natural sequence for writing, and students might profitably be assigned the entire sequence, working all term on a single project. They could try zero drafting from their sources, from contemplation, and from analysis. They could try developing their own analogies and exempla and drafting in dialogue. Then they could go step-by-step through the editorial procedures outlined in the second half of the book. On the other hand, the book can be used rather like a cookbook—which in many ways it is. Students could study and put to use only those parts of the book that bear directly on their special problems.

The book tries to be as honest as possible about the problems of drafting and basic editing. Most people think of drafting as simply writing down their thoughts readymade. They haven't learned to see drafting as a way of extending some thoughts and finding new ones. They need to know how a writer uses such things as sources and contemplation, analogies and analysis to keep his mind occupied with a topic long enough to produce the quantity of draft that is necessary to get one's best writing. Some students who draft easily but find editing difficult might safely ignore some of the chapters on drafting, but even they ought to read the chapters on tools and sources, for some of the advice in those chapters will make editing easier.

Most people think that editing is simply copy editing at its most rudimentary—checking spelling, usage, and punctuation. But the job entails much more. For an experienced writer, editing in its various forms is apt to make up more than half of the work of writing. It starts with sorting out and cutting apart the earliest draft. It includes summarizing, compressing, deleting, spot drafting, and organizing. Even students who believe they can edit easily ought to find the chapters on basic editorial procedures of value, if only because those chapters describe explicitly what a born editor does instinctively.

acknowledgments

Many people have helped us with this text, some unwittingly, others with much wit and good humor—especially the members of the rhetoric workshop at Yakima Valley College and the 1968–1969 teaching assistants in English at Central Washington State College. Leslie Balthazor, Vicki Stokes, John Ogmundson, and Phil Ternahan also deserve special mention. Our colleague, Kay Lybbert, gave aid and comfort to us as well as more precision to our ideas.

In the earliest phases of the project a brave woman bred by stout Finns, Sylvia Uusitalo, encouraged us and typed our drafts, again and again. In the later stages her colleague, Lorena Boersma, with great patience and good will, typed the final versions.

contents

introduction   xv

plans and drafts

1. THE ZERO DRAFT   3
    Seven De-Inhibitors   5
    The Use of Rituals   10

2. GETTING AT SOURCES   17
    The Prospectus   18
    On Source Material   19
    On Notes   26
    On Documentation   30
    On Style Manuals   33
    On Serendipity   34

3. HOW TOOLS CAN HELP   36
    On Paper   36
    The Loose-Leaf Binder System   37
    Getting the Words on Paper   41
    Using a Tape Recorder   42
    Books About Words   44

4. CONTEMPLATION: IMAGES AND TONES 47

    Images and Scenes   49
    On Making a Scene   50
    Empathy and Tone   53

5. HOW TO BE PRECISE 56

    Categories and Attributes   57
    Using the Idea Machine   64

6. THE DIALOGUE 66

    Choosing the Voices   67
    Choosing a Setting   69
    Dialogue Style   69
    Starting the Dialogue   70
    From Dialogue to Monologue   74
    A Note on Logic   75

7. HOW TO USE EXAMPLES AND ANALOGIES 76

    On Analogies   77
    Creating an Analogy   79
    Expanding an Analogy   82
    The Dictionary: A Source of Analogy   85
    Exempla: How to Use Them   87
    Two Final Suggestions   92

revisions

8. HOW TO GET FROM ZERO TO FIRST DRAFT 97

    Sorting the Draft   97
    Tentative Organization   99
    The First Draft   100
    The Commonplaces   100
    Zero Zero Draft   102

9. EDITING THE FIRST DRAFT: TOPICS AND SUMMARIES — 104

The Summary Sentence — 104
Sectioning the Draft — 106
Summary Sentences: Topics and Comments — 108

10. EDITING THE FIRST DRAFT: THE SENTENCE OUTLINE — 116

11. HOW TO CREATE A SENSE OF FORM — 120

Promises and Form — 121
How to Use Pro-Forms — 122

12. SEQUENCE, COHERENCE, AND TRANSITION — 126

How to Handle Semi-Coherent and Incoherent Draft — 128
On Transitions — 134

index — 137

introduction

There are two phases to writing. The first is called drafting; the other is called revising or editing. But though the two phases are distinct, they may alternate—and sometimes overlap. Some writers revise each batch of draft as it comes; others let draft accumulate. Sometimes the writer has no choice: In an essay examination the job must be done quickly, under pressure. Other times the writing can be more leisurely. But although approaches and jobs vary, there are habits and attitudes, procedures and concerns a writer can develop for each phase that support, rather than hinder, the other phase. Therefore, though this text breaks cleanly in half, the chapters on planning and drafting anticipate the revising phase, and the chapters on revising look back to the drafting phase.

Planning and drafting depend upon knowledge. A writer can only draft what he knows (or suspects). Although knowledge can come to a person inadvertently and incidentally, just because he lives and experiences things, the knowledge that a student most often writes from is acquired by study—that is, by borrowing the knowledge of others. At times the passive sponging-up of facts is appropriate for a writer, but most often he must grapple actively with the ideas of others. A writer can begin to draft from sources much earlier than most students realize. The early, almost immediate drafting that is described in the following chapters is the writer's way of grappling with and actively hooking his mind into the subject he is studying.

Many of the assignments in school demand that you know your own mind about a subject, so that your voice, when you speak and write of the subject, will be firm, controlled, and consistent. It will be the voice of one who knows how he stands, the voice of an individual committed in his own special way to the subject. Knowledge of your stance toward your subject comes through the intellectual act called "contemplation," and a chapter has been devoted to this kind of thinking. To call contemplation an "intellectual" act does not exclude the emotions. On the contrary, the prime virtue of contemplation is that it works only when the emotions are invoked.

Study and contemplation, then, form the basis for drafting. Study uses the experience of others; contemplation draws upon the emotions and images of personal experience.

The basis for editing is also knowledge, but of a special kind. The procedures described in the last half of this book are designed to yield a peculiar mixture of intimate, yet objective, knowledge. What was at first private thought is now becoming public. For a time the personal exploration of a topic is finished; the need now is for clarifying what has been discovered.

The ability to expand a thought and the ability to contract it are polar opposites; yet a good writer needs both abilities. He must be able to amplify a subject, to continue to draft until he has said enough —more than enough—about it. He must then be able to compress that thought into a compact sentence—even, at times, into a single, powerful phrase.

The phase of drafting is the phase of expansion, of amplification, of spreading out ideas and stretching them as far as possible. The editing phase is the phase of compression. Thus, the chapters on revising stress the technique of summarizing and the use of the compacted power of a summary sentence to give the reader a sense of control and form.

The jobs of drafting and editing demand mental sets that are quite different from one another—and neither can be held under complete conscious control. In drafting, momentum and flow are crucial; in editing, cutting and trimming. In drafting, the writer strives to involve himself intellectually and imaginatively in his material; in editing he must detach himself from it, coolly. The worries of drafting are different from those of editing. Premature revising can burden the job of drafting with worries that distract the mind and disrupt the flow of words and ideas. Premature revising can stifle drafting and thus destroy the very thing strong editing depends upon: extensive draft.

On the other hand, whether he is drafting or revising, much of the writer's work goes on beneath the surface of the mind, in the unconscious. When drafting, the writer courts insights that produce new avenues of thought, new sources of words and ideas—in short, those insights that lead to more draft. When revising, he courts insights that lead toward greater form. He looks for the new and unexpected connections that will pull heretofore disparate parts into a more coherent and unified whole. The insights hoped for in drafting and in editing are quite different, but they are the same in that, for the most part, they come out of an unconscious that is nourished and focused by an attentive, persistent conscious. Perhaps the basic lesson a writer can learn is to focus on the concerns of drafting until it is time to revise, remembering always that much of the best work is done more or less beyond conscious control.

writing: plans, drafts, and revisions

THE ZERO DRAFT

The initial product of the work of writing is not smoothly finished prose, a sentence outline, a "thesis statement," or even a rough draft. It is what Peter Drucker has called the " 'zero draft'— the one before the first." [1]

Zero draft is what a German would call *Stoff* —material, matter, substance . . . stuff. A sculptor starts with a pile of raw clay from which he can create a beautiful sculpture. The clay is the sculptor's *Stoff,* and the zero draft is the writer's version of the sculptor's raw clay. The zero draft is no more a rough draft of the final paper than is the raw clay a rough draft of the sculpture. Unlike a sculptor, a writer must create his own *Stoff*.

What is the ratio of zero draft to finished copy? The answer varies, but at the start try three to one. A finished paper of 500 words should have at least 1,500 words of zero draft—with perhaps 1,000 more words drafted during rewriting. Some jobs (and some writers) require a larger ratio of zero draft to finished copy, but as a rule of thumb try three to one. The more zero draft, the easier and better later writing will be. The more there is, the more you can throw away; and the more that can be thrown away, the better the chances that the remainder will be good. It is as simple as that. The best situation is to have, say, 10,000 words of draft and to know that 7,000 can be discarded. The worst situation is to need 3,000 words of final copy and to discover that you have run out of things to say after 1,000 words of drafting. Thus, a good part of this book deals with the problem of accumulating zero draft.

Zero draft can be accumulated in different ways. Drucker recommends a work schedule based upon effective use of what he calls "fairly large quantums of time":

> To write a report may, for instance, require six to eight hours. It is pointless to give seven hours to the task by spending fifteen minutes on it twice a day for three weeks. But if one can lock the door, disconnect the telephone, and wrestle with the report for five or six hours without interruption, one may come up with what I call a "zero draft"—the one before the first. Then one can rewrite section by section in small blocks of time.[2]

But not all writing chores demand that kind of schedule; neither would every writing problem nor would all writers submit to that procedure. Peter Drucker is a management consultant describing a kind of writing that is intellectual work under firm control. But much of a writer's (and a business manager's) best work goes on more or less beyond his immediate conscious control, deep within the unconscious mind. Productive thinking remains as yet a somewhat mysterious partnership between conscious and unconscious thought. But in general we do overrate the conscious mind and its contribution to creative thinking—and we underrate the unconscious. At times, especially for very long writing projects that are quite vague at the outset, a writer might just jot down notes that capture flashes of insight, clip ideas out of newspapers, draft short spurts of disconnected zero draft —never consciously quite sure where it is all leading. The French novelist Maurice Barrès wrote in this way. He would write notes in the middle of the night after awakening from a dream, or during a dreary session at Parliament, or after a long walk with his friend J. Tharaud, who described the results:

> These scattered fragments—of very uneven quality, brilliant ones making others seem thin and flat—comprised in the end a substantial, albeit shapeless, mass to which he gave a marvelously appropriate name. He called it his "monster."

"A monster! But a monster that exists. A shaggy reality, but one you can lean on." [3]

But probably for most students who are faced with the common kinds of writing one confronts in school—term papers, theses, and so forth—a third procedure is the most productive, one that combines Drucker's conscious control with Barrès' less controlled musing. A student needs a procedure that can accommodate scattered notes within scheduled quantums of time. He needs a procedure that will set his conscious mind on a job and yet encourage, even court, unconscious insights. It is this kind of procedure that is recommended and described in the following chapters.

Yet, whatever the procedure used to accumulate it, the initial product of the work of writing is normally the same—*Stoff*, a monster, zero draft.

SEVEN DE-INHIBITORS

Even professional writers blanch at the thought of starting a new writing job. Robert Crichton, the author of the novel *The Secret of Santa Vittoria*, put it with melancholy bluntness: "There is nothing in writing harder to do than to start." [4] So don't imagine that you are a "bad" writer simply because starting seems hard. In the early stage of drafting the major concerns are to get started and to keep writing. But there are a number of different worries and misconceptions that can effectively block a flow of ideas and words. The following seven admonitions are intended to encourage attitudes toward drafting that can disarm some of these worries and misconceptions, in order to remove some of the pain from the job of writing, and especially from the job of starting.

1. *Remember that you increase the likelihood of success if you think and act like an accomplished writer.* Very often students make their writing jobs needlessly forbidding by assuming that they are going to do badly. Such a pessimistic self-image might be understandable, since too often, after students write something, someone is there with a chart of correction symbols in one hand and a red pencil in the other ready to point out each and every failing. But, though under-

standable, pessimism is still not good, for if you expect failure, you will get it.

One basic secret of competency seems to be the knack of projecting a fore-image of success, in which one sees oneself doing the job and doing it well before the job is really begun. Athletes, especially, learn this lesson. Professional golfers, for instance, try to get a clear mental image of a shot before they actually make it. They imagine what it would look and feel like to make an absolutely perfect swing and to hit the ball just exactly where and how it should go. They have learned that if they can get that image clearly in mind, they stand a much better chance of a good shot than they do if they swing on the ball with no fore-image of success—or even worse, with a foreboding of failure: "I'm going to dump this thing into that pond. I just know it. . . ."

By the same token, the high jumper, before his jump, tries to see—and feel—himself going smoothly and perfectly over the bar. He calls it "psyching himself up." As part of getting ready, he envisions the job ahead in realistic detail and, most importantly, envisions doing it successfully. Suspicions of failure give way to images of competency. One should attend to how he can do the job well, rather than to how he might blunder.

The first advice for getting started and sustaining momentum, therefore, is to anticipate optimistically, and with as much realistic detail as possible, what it is like to be a competent writer. Think and feel like a winner and you at least increase the chances of being one.

2. *Remember that ignorance is no excuse.* Given any subject, you know enough about it to start drafting immediately. At the very least, you can describe the assignment, the state of your ignorance, and the plan of study necessary to become more expert. By writing this kind of prospectus, you begin to define and then to clarify the subject. (Chapter 2 discusses in more detail how to size up an assignment and how to use a prospectus to start drafting.) With a subject somewhat clarified and more firmly defined, you can examine your own memory and try to manifest the subject in a scene that can serve either as a focus for contemplation or as the basis for an analogy or example. (These techniques are discussed in more detail in Chapters 4 and 7.)

Even further, through that intricate filing system called "the English language," your mind stores more thoughts about and experiences with a given subject than might at first seem consciously obvious—even with a subject about which you might feel quite ignorant. Given any subject, you can immediately begin to analyze the language, or terms, you are already familiar with concerning it. You can, for instance, examine closely the basic terms you must use simply to describe it. (Chapter 5 offers some detailed help for this kind of analysis.) To keep writing, you need more ideas, but those ideas most often develop through writing; they come from trying to get half-formed, faintly developed notions onto a piece of paper. So do not fall victim to the false luxury of pleading ignorance in order to put off beginning to draft.

3. *Remember that you need not draft material in the order in which you finally present it to the reader.* A zero draft is not expected to have a beginning, middle, or end. Thus, in the privacy of a zero draft you can draft any part of the paper first. You don't have to worry about sequence of parts until the editing phase. Just get started drafting. Start at whatever point seems most attractive. And don't worry about making a detailed outline first. A simple scratch or box outline will do. In fact, at this early stage, having no outline at all probably would not hurt, for detailed outlines are only essential during the later editing job.

If you assume that a zero draft must somehow anticipate the final form of the paper, you accept some needless burdens. You may well spend much time staring at a blank sheet of paper, trying to figure out exactly how to start, how to cast that first beautiful sentence. Or you may not even be able to work up enough decisiveness to get out the blank sheet of paper, because you aren't exactly sure what to say. This kind of block grows out of the false assumption that an essay is drafted in one long, unbroken sequence, starting with the first graceful sentence, continuing through a firm and coherent middle, and then on to a resounding close. Actually, a writer can put together a finished paper in much the same way that a film editor puts together a finished movie—in bits and pieces. Openings are often written last. False starts are common. Smash endings are often originally buried in the middle of the zero draft. Thus a scissors is in every experienced writer's drawer, and thus, too, a special method for moving draft about and keeping track of it is described in Chapter 3.

The question of the drafting sequence has two sidelights that deserve special mention. First, sometimes a gap in knowledge looms up and threatens to stop a drafting session cold. The temptation is to quit writing and to go out to get more information. Perhaps you really will have to get more information eventually—one of the advantages of early drafting is that it exposes such weak spots in time to strengthen them. But don't stop a drafting session when such a gap appears. Instead, draft a description of the information needed and of where you can get it, and then go on with the drafting.

Second, sometimes you will draft until you reach a point that you have gone over time and again in the past. The prospect of replowing that tired old ground is nothing but an interruption and a bother to you. Or perhaps you have already written something but cannot find it immediately. At such points the main concern is to sustain that essential momentum—and it is precisely here that the "blah-blah" device can be useful. When faced with one of those miscellaneous interruptions, just write "blah-blah" and then go back to it later, after the momentum has been exhausted and you have a few minutes free to fill in the gap. Of course, if your draft begins running too heavy with "blah-blah's," it might be time to go to a movie.

4. *Don't be afraid to repeat ideas.* A photographer is allowed, even expected, to shoot an entire roll of film, taking the same subject over and over again from various angles in an attempt to get one good "take." When drafting, allow the same leeway and don't fear repetition. Get different "takes" of the subject. The only way to know the best way to say something is to try different ways of saying it. It may be that the first attempt is the best, but you cannot know that without trying other ways. When you can think of nothing to say, read over what you have already written and try to say it again differently, from a new camera angle, with different lighting. Do not be afraid to repeat again and again—not the same words, but the same ideas, the same material. During the editing phase you can compare the different versions and pick those that seem to be the best to present to the reader.

5. *Remember that words are cheap.* Words are probably the first thing that man learned to mass produce. Be prodigal with them—

at least in the early stages of drafting. Too much attention lavished on early words increases your personal investment in them, and makes it harder to throw them away later on: "I spent two hours getting that sentence just right, and, by God, now I'm not about to dump it." Such an attitude, though understandable, simply puts too high a price on early words. Keep the physical—and emotional—investment in your words low during early drafting, so that they will be easier to discard or replace during the editing phase.

6. *Always keep something in reserve for the next drafting session.* On projects of some length, every time the writer leaves the job and comes back to it, he faces the problem of beginning again. Many writers discover that the way they end a day's work can affect the way the work resumes, so they learn ways to end a session that make the start of the next one easier. They include as part of the closing ritual of each work session explicit plans on where they are going to start and what they are going to write next time. As Hemingway put it, "Write until you come to a place where you still have juice." [5] Robert Crichton describes the trick this way:

> There is a desire to finish a paragraph or a chapter and enjoy the satisfaction of finishing. It is a good feeling. But in the morning, there now is only that blank white sheet of paper to be filled. I have wasted days trying to regain a momentum I have lost. Now I don't allow myself the luxury of finishing. . . . When I am going good but have worked enough for the day, I stop before finishing a paragraph I am anxious to finish and then I stop in the middle of a sentence. It is irritating and frustrating but also effective.[6]

7. *Remember to keep first things first.* The job of accumulating zero draft can be much more difficult than it has to be if, in the privacy of drafting sessions, you worry about matters that are not actually important until later. Drafting is the process of keeping after what you want to say until you get it said; false starts and certain kinds of "mistakes" are inevitable—even valuable and necessary. Sentences that are not quite right, paragraph breaks that do not seem to be in the proper place, participles that are dangled, commas that are misplaced, the dreary business of *who* or *whom* and *between* or *among,* words that are misspelled—such sins are not to be worried

about while drafting. If you find them hard to ignore, perhaps the best thing to do is to commit them—and stop worrying. Follow Martin Luther's advice: "Be a sinner and sin boldly." Deliberately misspell a few words and dangle a participle or two.

The zero draft offers marvelous opportunity for an orgy of taboo-breaking. Almost any sin can be enjoyed in the privacy of an early draft with no risk of public scandal. Later, during the editing phase, you can quietly remove the really scandalous sins. Thus, by keeping editorial concerns out of the private domain of drafting, you can enjoy a few sins—and later, as editor, you can enjoy the prissy pleasures of the public censor.

But cultivating too early a critical editor's spirit will inhibit drafting. Besides, more often than not an early draft is better than it looks at first, and premature criticism demands things of it that should not yet be demanded.

In a very real sense this last suggestion, to keep first things first, is the most important of the seven. It is implicit in just about everything that will be said in this book. The two quite different jobs of writing—drafting and editing—ought to be kept distinct. To attempt to do both at once is to risk doing both badly.

THE USE OF RITUALS

Anything that can lessen the sense of unfamiliarity with the role of writer will reduce the difficulties of starting and restarting to write. One powerful help can be to find ways to ritualize the job of writing. A ritual involves a prescribed or established procedure of gestures and words that are prefabricated for certain occasions. A ritual—the repetition of motions planned and performed beforehand—can lend a job enough familiarity to encourage self-confidence.

Ritualized ways of beginning focus your nervous and intellectual energy on a particular job by eliminating some minor distracting choices that might otherwise have to be made. Your ritual may be as simple as sharpening all of your pencils or reaching for a special pad of paper. It may be more complex—straightening out your desk before starting, or fixing a cup of coffee that will stand and get cold. Or it may be even more elaborate—going to a special place at a special time, using special tools, or giving in to certain quirks and idiosyncrasies. But, simple or complex, the ritual should become the habitual signal that work is about to be done. As such, the ritual should prepare the mind to release what Brewster Ghiselin calls its "unorganized riches." [7]

Choosing a Time

A basic—if somewhat unexciting—part of the ritual is setting up a schedule. The exact number and length of the writing sessions depends finally on your other commitments and your metabolism. The point is that writing takes more time than is usually allotted it, and scheduling is the only way to guarantee that time.

Probably it is best *not* to say something like, "From now on, all term long, I am going to write at three o'clock every Tuesday, Thursday, and Saturday afternoons for two hours." So rigid a schedule is almost impossible to maintain, and when it doesn't work, it leads too easily to frustration and needless discouragement. But just as you can plan for two or three days ahead of time to see a movie at seven o'clock on Saturday evening, so you can make an appointment with yourself a day or two ahead of time for a writing session at a specified hour. You must learn to promise yourself the time you need one, two, or three days in advance—but then you must follow through and use that time for your writing.

Because of this need for scheduling, most writers work when they can count on fairly long stretches of uninterrupted time, which means they tend to do their drafting in the early mornings or in the late evenings. But there is a hidden advantage to drafting during those quiet times: Distractions are fewer and inhibitions weaker. Fatigue or drowsiness relax the guards of consciousness and can make you more receptive to the creative powers of the unconscious. Thus many creative people seem consistently to do their best thinking late in the evening, very often after they are in bed and are not quite asleep. They often have to postpone sleep until the fresh thoughts have been drafted. Others have their new insights early in the morning before they are fully awake and moving about. A "morning person," like Bruce Catton, wakes early and does his most creative work before his regular office hours begin. Inspiration is still a mystery, but enough creative people believe it favors the twilight times of late evening or early morning to make these times worth considering when scheduling time to write.

In a less secular, more religious age the source of fresh, fertile, creative insights was believed to be a Muse, a goddess who was especially fond of forests and glades. Today the Muse is said to reside in that mysterious part of the mind called "the unconscious." But wherever she conceals herself, she is worth courting, because the unaided conscious mind, restricted as it is by established shapes and patterns, seldom comes up with a new idea or a new shape and pattern for experience. Arthur Koestler suggests well the limitations of the conscious mind in his book *The Act of Creation:*

> The prerequisite of originality is the art of forgetting, at the proper moment, what we know. . . . Without the art of forgetting, the mind remains cluttered up with ready-made answers, and never finds occasion to ask the proper questions.[8]

New ideas emerge from the unconscious with a curious suddenness and unpredictability. They are notorious for the way they ignore schedules. The main insight for Einstein's theory of relativity came to him suddenly as he was getting out of bed. Poincaré, the French mathematician, reports that one day the solution to a difficult and important problem came into his mind unexpectedly and with absolute precision and clarity just as he was stepping onto a bus. New ideas can come when they are the least expected—just as you get up from the dinner table, just as you step into the shower, just before you start work, or just before you fall asleep.

On the other hand, the unconscious will not take care of things entirely by itself. It needs nourishment and it needs prodding. It is nourished by reading and thinking and talking and writing about your subject, by filling your mind, conscious and unconscious, full of your subject. The unconscious is prodded by tightening the tension between it and the conscious mind, by setting the conscious mind to firmly scheduled, deliberate tasks that will keep it focused on the material under study. The devices described in Chapters 4 through 7 and the editorial techniques described in Chapters 8 through 10 can provide good bones for the conscious mind to gnaw on while the unconscious is doing its work.

There is a kind of fruitful distraction of the conscious that opens the door of the entire mind. While the door remains open, much that is not conscious also is revealed. Often the richest of insights expose themselves by slipping in at the edges of awareness, while the conscious mind stubbornly pursues its dogged path.

Because the Muse is coy, insights often will not present themselves immediately after tedious and strenuous mental efforts, but only after a release from scheduled work. Brewster Ghiselin describes the phenomenon this way in his book *The Creative Process:*

> Though the tension of conscious striving tends to overdetermine psychic activity, to narrow and fix it, such tension gives stimulation and direction to the unconscious activity which goes on after the tension is released. The desired developments are usually delayed for some time, during which presumably something like incubation is going on and attention may be profitably turned to something else. Then without warning the solution or the germinal insight may appear.[9]

If students seldom experience moments of insight, it may be because they ignore the pattern the Muse prefers—strenuous courting, then rest. Putting the job off until the final weeks of a term, rushing through drafts, avoiding the discipline of a schedule—these are not ways to court inspiration. The Muse will not be rushed. She demands her time. Eventually—again, usually when least expected—there will come that breakthrough, that "ah ha!" marking an insight. Because of this unconscious factor, because conscious effort is not in itself enough, be alert and ready to capture those fugitive ideas when they do come into your conscious mind. Get them down on paper or tape or something, so that you will have them and can return to them later to work out the details—as Barrès did with his monster. The binder system described in Chapter 3 is quite helpful for keeping track of those fugitive ideas.

Getting Set Up

Arranging yourself and your tools into a routine pattern is another bit of ritual that can make the job of writing more familiar and therefore less formidable. It is probably best to be reasonably comfortable, but not too relaxed, cool rather than too warm. If you have found a place that can be devoted solely to intellectual work, fine; but try to avoid becoming addicted to one special place. In time your work habits should become more ritualized and comfortable, but they should stay flexible and realistic—and even mobile. Instead of a special place, think rather of a ritualistic setup, one that is portable and depends upon a certain frame of mind, a collection of familiar tools, and a few minimal, though essential, conditions.

The choice of a few minimal but essential conditions raises the question of distractions and noise. Students sometimes insist to themselves that they must have absolute quiet and absolutely no distractions to do their writing. But such an ideal is almost impossible to attain. Sometimes, in fact, people find that if they deprive themselves of familiar noises, they are apt to begin to hear their own hearts beat and the sound of their blood rushing through their brains—situations usually not conducive to intellectual effort. Recently two students described what seemed to be realistic conditions for quiet: "The best condition is the apartment living room, where the sounds are steady and *familiar* to me. The bathroom would do just as well, but there is less space there and no table." "I find it easiest to work in my single room in the dorm. I turn on my radio to drown the noise of my neighbors. My own noise doesn't seem to bother me."

Many students find that they need a certain communal support in order to write most comfortably. They seem to work better where they can actually see others at work. Thus some students find that they do their best work in places such as the library or the study room in a dormitory: "I work better in the library. With other people around me working, I feel like maybe I'm working. I guess I borrow some enthusiasm from the others, or a contagion." "I work best in the study room with others around me, but no one to talk to." Even with a job so notoriously lonely as writing, the condition of solitude must be kept flexible enough to match your own personal needs with the practical choices available to you.

People—especially friends—are important to the writer in other ways, too. A writer needs all sorts of props for his confidence. He needs friends close-by, for friends can encourage good work simply by believing in him and his ability. They may not be reliable editors, because they are apt to overlook flaws and to gush enthusiastically, but so long as you take care not to believe all the good things they say and listen carefully to their criticisms, your friends can give the moral support and encouragement that can make the job of writing less painful.

Another way a writer can comfortably set himself up to write is by giving in to his idiosyncrasies. An idiosyncrasy is a habit or mannerism that is peculiar to an individual. Thus, for the people who have them, idiosyncrasies are as familiar as a favorite pair of slippers—old, maybe, but comfortable. Most authors find that they write more confidently if they give in to certain idiosyncrasies. Some—Proust and Twain, for instance—found that they wrote best in bed. Some, like Thomas Wolfe, preferred to write standing up. The German poet Schiller is reported to have preferred writing at a desk with rotten apples in it; the smell apparently inspired him. The French novelist Balzac preferred writing while wearing monk's robes. There are reports—perhaps apocryphal—that Karl Marx preferred writing with his feet in a pan of cold water.

Some students have found that they prefer writing in their underwear. One of our colleagues can compose best with a favorite pen filled with a certain shade of blue ink. Another can write best if he uses many qualifying adverbs in his early draft; the adverbs seem to make him more comfortable by hedging and qualifying the sometimes outrageous things he says. Another has found that he can write best if he intersperses his early draft with sometimes irrelevant observations on what he considers the more fuzzy-headed practices of some of his colleagues. We have even heard of one young woman who preferred stripping down and wrapping herself in a large velvet cloth for her writing sessions.

The list of idiosyncrasies is endless, but the upshot of it all is simple: Do not be afraid to exercise any familiar quirks that might help you maintain a flow of ideas and words, especially during the early stages of drafting. It does not really matter what the idiosyncrasy is, so long as it doesn't bother other people too much and is something you can indulge in freely—and so long as you don't become unrealistically addicted to it. Cultivate your quirks—just enough to help establish a useful ritual and just enough to make the role of writer more familiar.

Closely related to the exercise of idiosyncrasies is another, sometimes helpful, device, one often used by people who are attempting to quit smoking cigarettes: Don't be afraid to pamper yourself a little bit. Don't be afraid to reward yourself with little treats that you allow yourself only during writing sessions: an expensive brand of tea or coffee, a special confection, a favorite picture or trinket on your desk, a certain kind of music. Such things, trivial as they might seem to be, can do much to take the pain out of the role of writer, especially during the terrible starts.

NOTES

1. Peter Drucker, "How to Manage Your Time," *Harper's Magazine,* 233 (December 1966), 60.
2. Drucker, p. 60.
3. Quoted in Jean Guitton, *A Student's Guide to Intellectual Work,* trans. Adrienne Foulke (Notre Dame, Ind.: University of Notre Dame Press, 1965), p. 55.
4. Robert Crichton, "The Real Secret of Santa Vittoria," *Playboy,* 15 (November 1968), 196.
5. Ernest Hemingway, in *Writers at Work: The Paris Review Interviews,* 2nd series (New York: Viking, 1965), p. 221.
6. Crichton, p. 196.
7. Brewster Ghiselin, "Introduction," *The Creative Process* (New York: New American Library, 1958), p. 25.
8. Arthur Koestler, *The Act of Creation* (New York: Dell, 1967), p. 190.
9. Ghiselin, p. 29.

GETTING AT SOURCES 2

Most of the writing done in schools is in the form of reports, which is a species of journalism. The student-writer is like a reporter who goes out seeking a story by asking questions. Indeed, most of the disciplines studied in school can be viewed as special ways of asking questions. For instance, the historian of the Napoleonic wars questions the artifacts—the literate residue of the events of the period—in order to better understand the people of the period. The social psychologist might question the machine-scored answer sheets of a questionnaire. With his testing procedures the chemist questions the substances he is studying and then interprets the results of the tests. The point is that the primary source of information is not the thing being questioned, but rather the questioning itself. Things don't yield information; questions do.

Questions are the form that thought takes at the start of research. The form it takes as research continues is the "hypothesis." The hypothesis is a natural extension of the question: It is, in fact, a tentative answer to it. It is wise to approach source material of any kind with a set of hypotheses already formed, but also with a profound willingness to modify or discard and replace any hypothesis that proves untenable. A hypothesis is tentative—and discardable. When it ceases to hold water, you throw it away. Since a hypothesis exists only to have its adequacy tested, any inhibitions you might have stemming from the common fear of "making a mistake" have to be overcome. If a hypothesis proves to be inadequate, which it well might, try again with a new hypothesis. Out of the abortive attempt a more sound hypothesis will most likely develop.

The basic energy units of real research, therefore, are the thoughtful question and the discardable hypothesis. Even before you start reading, put into writing the ideas your mind already has for exploring your subject:

> What do you already know?
> What questions can you ask of your subject?
> How do you go about finding answers to such questions?
> What sort of tentative answers, or hypotheses, can you, yourself, propose?

THE PROSPECTUS

You can make the answers to these four questions somewhat more solid and real by borrowing a device from the professional writer, who often uses a "prospectus," or a query letter, to see if his ideas and skills are marketable. A prospectus that receives a favorable response from an editor can give the writer not only solid advice on his project, but also a sense of assurance that his work will be considered with care and will receive serious editorial attention.

There are also some real advantages for you, the student, in turning over a prospectus to your instructor as soon as possible after a writing job has been assigned. For one thing, a prospectus will start you thinking about your project immediately. It can also provide you with an initial, sometimes surprising, opinion from your instructor, who can often suggest tactics and sources of information, can warn of pitfalls, and in general can play the role of sympathetic editor. A prospectus is a sales pitch and, as such, it must convince the instructor that what is being proposed is worth doing and that it is within your competency.

The prospectus should answer the kind of questions an editor would ask, such as:

What is the angle you have in mind?
With what material do you intend to work?
How competent are you?
Why are you interested?
Who are the experts in the field and how well do you know their work?
What readers would be interested in such a study, and why?

In short, tell everything you can think of about your relationship to your subject. For this first phase of the writing job you might try out the notion of overproduction discussed in the previous chapter; try to draft about three times as much material as you think you will finally need, then cut it back.

ON SOURCE MATERIAL

Because the average college library holds so much material—good, bad, mediocre, relevant, irrelevant—it could take too much time to sort out what you need without help. At least at first you will find it helpful to concentrate on up-to-date, book-length studies written by people who have read and analyzed the material published about your subject.

The Ideal Starter Text

The first book you read is especially important. It will occupy a great deal of your time and it will establish many of your attitudes. So it should be selected carefully. The ideal starter text should have the following characteristics:

1. *It should be relevant.* The text should not only speak about the subject you are studying, but should place it in the larger context of the issues and patterns surrounding it. For instance, if your subject is the transcendental philosophy of Ralph Waldo Emerson, you will want a starter text that discusses the forerunners and the descendants of that philosophy as well as the philosophy itself.

2. *It should be authoritative.* It should be written by someone whose information and judgment can be trusted, and it must be writ-

ten in sufficient detail to give some idea of the complexities of the matter. Trying to decide whether an author is an authority and a book reliable is a problem only when the subject is new to you. If you are expert or even semi-expert, you know who is best and you can recognize reliable information. To do so is the mark of expertness. But there are ways for newcomers to gain some assurance about an author and his information. These ways are described later in the chapter.

3. *It should be readable.* Remember that readability is a relative thing, that what is readable to an expert in the field might be unintelligible to you. Progress in a discipline is marked by the precision and complexity of the questions one can ask and handle. Those who know most in any given field are those who can ask and cope with the most precise and complex questions. At the start of a project, while you are still something of a novice, avoid those books that are so technical and specialized that they will engulf you in complexities. Start with more general material and work toward more specialized studies. Quite likely by the end of a project you will be able to handle with relative ease fairly technical studies, but at the outset it is best to work with a book that does not consistently frustrate and mystify you with its technicalities.

4. *It should be current.* For most writing projects, you will want to begin with a book that incorporates recent work in your field.

5. *It should have some sort of bibliography.* Early in the research of your project a bibliography is especially essential, for it can help you separate the good from the bad published material. You will need help finding out who is who among the experts, and a selective bibliography from an authority in the field is a good place to start. The bibliography sometimes appears as a single list titled "Bibliography" or "Further Reading" or some such phrase. Sometimes there are only bibliographical footnotes that can be used with an index. The ideal bibliography at this stage is one that is annotated—that is, offers a brief description and sometimes an evaluation of each book.

How to Find Source Material

Sometimes you will find a book that satisfies all five criteria, but just as often your ideal starter text will have to be a composite of several works, perhaps gathered in loose-leaf fashion from chapters of books, lecture notes, and articles and periodicals.

Periodical Guides. The criterion of currency is the one that is apt to force you to use the periodicals. But periodicals should be used only when your subject demands it. For many subjects, "currency" does not mean "last month" or even "last year." For example, with a subject such as medieval warfare a book written seventy years ago is still "current." For such subjects stick to books and make use of a guide like Winchell's (see pages 24–26). On the other hand, with a subject like "the latest Middle Eastern crisis" current magazines and the more reliable newspapers are sources that must necessarily be used. And the guides to such sources are, then, invaluable. The three most common guides are *The International Index, The Reader's Guide to Periodical Literature,* and *The New York Times Index.* (For local and regional events, ask your librarian if there is an index available for the larger regional newspapers.) Remember the problems in using the material listed in these guides. For one thing, they cover too much material that is too often not authoritative. It is important that you do not allow yourself to get mired down in a great mass of articles from popular magazines; such articles simply use up too much of your time, tend to be repetitive and too thin in content, and are not always very authoritative.

One good rule of thumb is to avoid unsigned articles in periodicals. An unsigned article is like an unsigned check: There may be something backing it up, but without the name on the line, it doesn't mean much. Another good rule of thumb is to try, as soon as possible, not to concentrate on the popular magazines, but to use the more weighty sources discussed later in this chapter.

The Card Catalog. The place to start a search for a book-length study is the library's card catalog. Books are listed in the catalog in three ways: by author, by title, and by subject matter. If you are starting from scratch, of course, the author and title listings will not be too helpful, so look up your subject in the catalog. If you do not find it, place your subject in a more inclusive category and look there. For instance, if you are writing about harmonicas, it is quite likely that you will not find the heading "Harmonicas" in the catalog. The next largest category would be something like "Musical Instruments" and this would be a likely subject to look under.

Working with a card catalog is a little like eating potato chips, for once you get started it's very easy to keep going. Sometimes it may be difficult to get started, so don't be afraid to ask a librarian to help you.

The card catalog contains much information about a book, such as how current it is and whether it includes a bibliography. The catalog card also indicates what other subject headings the book is listed under. This information is particularly helpful if the subject heading you start with in the catalog does not seem to provide enough promising titles. In such a case, simply cast about through the catalog, following the leads provided by the cross references under subject headings. These other subject headings might well list some books that, though not listed under the heading you started with, are relevant to your subject. These cross references are printed on the card just above the little hole at the bottom.

Examining the Books

Once you have some promising titles, examine the books themselves. As you examine each book for its relevance, authoritativeness, and readability, start accumulating zero draft by writing down your judgments of each book. Start each examination by looking carefully at the table of contents, introduction, and preface to get an idea of the book's range and shape and, hence, relevance. Also, check its index for terms that apply to your subject; see if there is a bibliography, and read a bit here and there in the book, to get some sense of how readable it is. Skim the book—especially the opening and closing paragraphs of chapters and opening and closing sentences of paragraphs within the chapters—to get an idea of the contents and readability.

You now should have checked four of the five criteria: the book's relevance, readability, currency, and whether it has a bibliography. It remains to see how authoritative and reliable the author is.

Examining the Author. To help determine how authoritative an author is, check such biographical reference books as the *Dictionary of American Biography, Current Biography, Directory of American Scholars, American Men of Letters, American Men of Science,* and, for British writers, *Dictionary of National Biography.* Also check in one of the volumes of *Who's Who.* Separate volumes list different groups of people, such as historians, musicians, members of certain ethnic groups, residents of certain areas of the country, and so forth. Another handy aid is Constance M. Winchell's *Guide to Reference Books,* an extremely helpful book that will be discussed in more detail later in this chapter. Under "Biography" in the index to the *Guide,* you will find a long list of specialized biographical reference books, at least one of which will probably offer some information on the writer whose scholarly stature you are interested in checking.

Another fairly helpful technique for checking authoritativeness is to play off one author against another. To get some idea about who the most respected writers are, check the sources in the bibliographies and indexes of the books you have selected to see what the authors say about one another. But the most help in this final winnowing out of titles comes from the reviews published in the scholarly journals—reviews of scholars by scholars for scholars. These reviews give some indication of how the book was received by the experts. A good review will also give some insight into the present, overall shape of a subject area and will nearly always include reference to related books and articles. One warning: Reviewers often tend to disagree among themselves, so don't necessarily trust the first one you read.

Short of asking a local expert (perhaps a member of the faculty), the best way to find the book reviews you want is to make use of the following three publications, all of which stay up-to-date: *Book Review Digest, Book Review Index,* and *An Index to Book Reviews in the Humanities.* Check one or more of these sources for the year in which the book was first published and for two or three years thereafter. There is sometimes a considerable lag between publication and review in a scholarly journal.

Getting Help from Professors. When checking to see whether a source is authoritative, the sensible thing to do is to ask the advice of someone who is an authority himself—a professor in the field, for instance. A college campus represents a large collection of experts, and you should not feel shy about putting them to use. You may have to make a couple of tries at locating a willing professor, but it is well worth perseverance.

Before you approach a professor for help be sure you have made a trip to the library and checked out a couple of likely-looking titles to ask his advice about. Approach him with a plan for writing about the subject—ideally a prospectus such as the one described earlier. Explain, as best you can, your present level of competency, and ask him which of the books you have found he would recommend as a starter, or, if none seems right, what other book or books he would recommend. If he discourages your initial aims, ask him what he believes would be an appropriate set of questions for you to begin with—and weigh his advice very carefully.

Winchell's Guide to Reference Books. The periodical literature published each year in the various academic fields is overwhelming—not only in its sheer bulk, but, distressingly, often in its mind-sticking mediocrity. Approach this scholarly periodical literature cautiously—as you would the edge of a swamp—and use a bibliography, preferably one that is annotated and up-to-date. Most helpful here are the current bibliographical surveys for the various fields and the regular (usually annual) bibliographies that list current articles and books in special fields. These surveys and annual bibliographies appear either in certain journals or else as separate publications. But trying to wend your way through the many bibliographies, and bibliographies of bibliographies, and bibliographies of bibliographies of bibliographies can be a confusing, frustrating experience. Perhaps the best advice is simply to get to know Constance M. Winchell's *Guide to Reference Books*, 8th ed. (Chicago: American Library Association, 1968). Winchell's *Guide* is a very detailed and up-to-date description of very nearly all of the basic reference works available. The major areas covered are:

A. General Reference

B. Humanities
    Applied Arts   Linguistics and Philology
    Fine Arts   Literature

Music   Religion
Philosophy   Theater Arts

C. Social Science
 General Works   Law
 Anthropology and Ethnology Mythology
 Economics   Political Science
 Education   Sociology
 Folklore and Popular Customs Statistics
 Geography

D. History and Area Studies
 General History
 Africa   Australia and New
 The Americas   Zealand
 Arctic and Antarctic Europe
 Asia   Oceanica

E. Pure and Applied Sciences
 General Works   Engineering
 Agricultural Sciences Mathematics
 Astronomy   Medical Sciences
 Biological Sciences   Physics
 Chemistry   Psychology and
 Earth Sciences   Psychiatry (including
         Occultism)

Within each area (and there are a number of finer subdivisions not listed above), the reference works are classified by types, with a description of what each one attempts to do.

 First, check the *guides* for your subject. A guide is a basic bibliography, hopefully annotated, that often provides critical judgments of the basic works in the field and suggests procedures for conducting library research. After the guides, you should check the *bibliographies,* the *indexes* (which list periodical articles, book reviews, and essays in collections), the *abstracts* (which list and summarize different kinds of publications), and the specialized *encyclopedias* and *dictionaries.* If your subject does not fall into one of the special areas listed in Winchell's *Guide,* check the first section of the book, which deals with general reference works; check especially the periodical indexes listed there.

Winchell's *Guide* can give you an overview of the basic reference material relevant to a project—and it can save an immense amount of time. In general, the sooner you become acquainted with this book and start putting it to use, the better.

ON NOTES

You cannot really begin to know whether or not the book you have chosen is the right one until you have read it. So start reading. If at first the book doesn't seem to be supplying what you need, jump ahead in it, for many books start slowly. If it still doesn't seem to be on the mark, jump ahead some more. If it still doesn't seem to make it, try another book.

Taking Notes

In the following two sentences Richard Altick cuts through a great deal of the curious nonsense that is sometimes prescribed concerning methods of note taking:

> No two persons make research notes exactly the same way, and there is, in fact, no absolutely "right" or "wrong" way to do so. The two goals are efficiency and accuracy, and whatever methods achieve them for the individual scholar are wholly legitimate.[1]

Try a variety of note-taking techniques until you find the one that suits you best.

So far as format is concerned, the backs of envelopes will work if there is nothing else available. Three-by-five-inch cards are widely used and are handy if you don't want to carry around a stenographer's note pad or legal tablet or ring binder. The loose-leaf binder system described on pages 37–41 will allow you to take notes on whatever is handy just as long as it can be glued, stapled, or taped to a loose-leaf backing sheet, which can be filed in a standard three-ring binder. Naturally, if you are going to be stapling or gluing notes to backing sheets in a binder, you ought to remember to write on just one side. But once again, the actual form for notes is a matter of personal preference.

If much of your note taking is from oral sources—lectures, discussions, interviews—a portable tape recorder might be useful. See pages 42–44 for a discussion of some of the techniques and problems involved in using tape recorders.

Remember Altick's observation that the two goals are efficiency and accuracy. Whatever procedure you finally work out, it must include a reliable and efficient system for indicating the source of a note. Such information is distressingly easy to forget, and there are few things more discouraging than working with a set of notes from sources that you can no longer identify.

Here is a simple system that students have found useful: On every writing project, maintain a permanent numbered list of sources, numbering each one as you go. Fasten your list to a special set of backing sheets—extra heavy (the end sheets in a package of binder filler work fine, and so do those sets of loose-leaf indexes). Keep the backing sheets permanently in the loose-leaf binder assigned to the writing project at hand. As you use a source, jot down an exact and complete reference note for it, promptly; then number it and add it to the list. The essential information needed consists of the author, the title, the exact pages involved, and the crucial publication information (for books: place of publication, publisher, and date; for articles: name of the periodical, volume number, and date).

With this system any source material can be identified simply by number. For example, suppose you are writing about modern poetry and have listened to and taken notes on Robert Lowell's tape-recorded conversation with Cleanth Brooks and Robert Penn Warren. Suppose that you habitually have made bibliographic notes of your sources on three-by-five-inch cards. (It is not essential that you use three-by-five-inch cards for each of your sources, for the loose-leaf system will accept items in a variety of forms, but there are real advantages to using the cards: They are pocket size, they are sturdy, and they can be removed from the backing sheet and rearranged in alphabetical order when you make up the final bibliography for your final draft.) And, finally, suppose that this is the fourth source you have used. The card on Lowell's conversation would be entered on the list as shown in Figure 1. The notes from this source need only be marked with the circled number 4 plus a careful indication of the exact pages covered by that note. Each separate note from that source subsequently will bear that same number 4. No matter how widely you

28 plans and drafts

> Vachek, Josef ① P 121 V28
> The Linguistic School of Prague: An
> Introduction to its Theory & Practice
> Bloomington & London: Indiana U., 1966
>
> ② Lecture notes –
> Prof. O.Q. Martin
>
> ③ Ohmann, Richard
> "Generative Grammars and the Concept of Literary Style"
> Word, XX (1964), 423–439
>
> ④ Robert Lowell
> With Cleanth Brooks and Robert Penn Warren
> Conversation on the Craft of Poetry
> (tape recording, tape #2)
> New York: Holt, Rinehart, & Winston, 1961.

FIGURE 1. A list of sources, numbered and filed on a loose-leaf backing sheet

scatter the notes throughout a manuscript, their number will quickly identify their source.

Notes as Zero Draft

With new, unfamiliar material a thoughtful reader finds himself taking notes that are often direct quotations from the text. As the reader learns more about the subject, the notes begin to be summaries of what he reads and soon include questions and statements of disagreement. This paraphrasing, summarizing, and questioning of source material is a form of zero drafting. Start drafting in this way just as soon as you begin to get the gist of a source's argument—and start with your very first source.

In your reading notes keep track of which comments are paraphrases and summaries of the material and which are your own commentaries on the material. Put the personal commentaries between double parentheses, or switch from pen to pencil or from black to red lead. But be sure to keep yourself honest about which ideas you got from the source and which ideas are yours.

Remember that even as you paraphrase and summarize things you have read or heard, your mind will impress itself on the material. It will classify and organize the material given to it. You may be surprised at how much your mind works at its own organization. And one of the things you always want to notice is what your own mind, consciously or unconsciously, is doing to the material with which it is working.

As you progress in your reading and study you will rely on direct quotation less and less. There are usually only two reasons why you would quote material directly. First, if a passage says something so well that a paraphrase would dilute its effect, then quote it. But do not let this escape clause tempt you into passively copying out passage after passage. Second, if a passage says something you feel is important, but you do not yet fully understand it, it is safer to quote it than to paraphrase it. In a case like this, which is not at all uncommon, note the passage, but don't take the time to copy it immediately. Instead, keep a list of the pages that contain those troublesome, but important, passages. Then, when finished with the book, go back and read the passages again. Very often passages that seemed opaque at first will be quite clear later. Those that still bother you should be copied for further mulling.

Photocopying

Photocopying can save time and can increase the accuracy of one's use of sources. There are times when you might want to copy a long, long quotation verbatim from a text. It can be photocopied at most libraries for a dime or so. A photocopy machine is perhaps most useful for copying maps, complex tables, and charts—in short, those graphic devices that can otherwise present overwhelming difficulties for the memory and the records. Remember, too, to identify the exact source on the copy. (Just a circled number will do it, if you use the system described a few pages back.)

In general, any mechanical device that can ease some of writing's physical chores should be welcome. Admittedly, some writers still avoid such contraptions, but then it took time to get used to the invention of mass-produced books; and the introduction of the pencil was probably rather a shock to some scholars, too. Try any device available to you, but feel free, too, to ignore any that seem to get in the way of the ultimate job—writing. The moral is that mechanical aids can make it easier to involve yourself more fully with your material. The energy and time saved by mechanization can be wisely invested in the more demanding, more subtle, more creative, and, finally, more important aspects of the job—that is, the more human and creative aspects that cannot be mechanized.

ON DOCUMENTATION

Footnotes and bibliography, the mechanisms for documentation, differ in intent and form from discipline to discipline, and from journal to journal. The needs of the literary critic writing for *The New York Review of Books* are not those of the electronic engineer writing for the *I.R.E. Journal*. The two journals represent different traditions of documentation. The first tradition grew out of a primarily religious and ethical desire to identify and refer to exact lines in texts—because the texts were the sacred words of God or of some lesser lawgiver. The second tradition grew out of a primarily scientific need to refer back not to exact lines but to entire experiments or recipes. In general today, the first tradition is dominant in the humanities—and in administrative bureaucracy; the second is dominant in the natural and behavioral sciences—and in cookbooks.

There is a dual need at the base of the religious tradition of documentation: the need to preserve, unaltered, a text whose language became more unfamiliar as time passed, and the need to explain and explicate particular passages of the text. These two needs produced systems of documentation in which any line or verse or paragraph of a text could be referred to unambiguously. It was to meet these needs, for example, that Biblical scholars numbered lines and established verses and chapters in the Old and New Testaments. Today, the need for this kind of documentation exists in secular affairs, too. The literary critic needs to be able to refer to exactly the relevant line or verse or paragraph in a reliable text. The historian and philosopher have much the same need. And just as the Biblical scholar must be able to refer to a reliable and precise passage from a divine source, the lawyer also must be able to refer quickly, reliably, and precisely to some legal precedent as established by a judge or lawgiving body. So, too, must the military or civilian bureaucrat, who is concerned with previous policy statements, memoranda, and directives coming down through the apparatus of social control.

The second tradition of documentation stems more or less from the medieval alchemists, those forerunners of today's chemists and physicists. As with a young housewife preparing her first casserole, they needed to be able to refer back to a total experiment or recipe, to the detailed procedures involved, and to the results. Today, scientific writing, especially in the natural and behavioral sciences, has this same need. As a result, most scientific writing today begins with a *review of the literature,* which identifies and usually comments upon the previous work that has been done in the field and brings the reader up to the particular problem under discussion.

The two traditions can still be found in their pure forms—the religious-ethical, for instance, in law briefs and books of poetry criticism; the scientific, in reports on natural science and engineering and in cookbooks. But there is also considerable mixing of the traditions —most noticeably in the social sciences where the passage of time and the proliferation of idiosyncrasies have produced a mare's-nest of documentations with mixed intents and differing forms. This confusion in some academic areas can make life miserable for the beginning scholar especially, but some general guidelines can make things less confusing.

The basic point of all documentation is something that is common to both of the original traditions. Documentation is basically an appeal to previous statements. Apparently since the beginning of human argument man has found that one useful way to strengthen his case is to find a previous "somebody else," especially an important "somebody else," who agrees with him or whose previous work supports his current endeavors. The religious scholar's appeal to the exact word of God and the scientist's appeal to a reputable earlier experiment are both appeals to authority. Anytime you find yourself saying, "According to so-and-so," you are using that appeal to authority.

Much documentation represents an appeal to authority. Earlier in this chapter we suggested ways to immerse yourself in authoritative materials. Documentation is the residue of that immersion in authority. From a social point of view, documentation is a form of acceptable name-dropping. Done with restraint and discretion, it can lend your writing an aura of stability and prestige. Overdone, it becomes heavy-handed and tedious—like the conversation of the pompous windbag who keeps telling you about all of his celebrity friends.

Another major use of documentation is to provide a record of your reading in the field; it lets a reader know that you know who is who in the field. It becomes, that is, a sort of appeal to *your* authority. Further, documentation suggests lines of inquiry for a reader to pursue, should he desire to read more deeply on the subject. So your documentation can serve exactly the same function for a reader that your sources' documentation served for you: It can help guide him through the morass of publications in the field.

Finally, footnoting is a useful way to pay debts. A footnote helps put the credit—or blame—where it belongs. If you have made use of somebody's facts or opinions—facts that he worked hard to accumulate and that have not yet become commonly enough known to be in the public domain—then indicate your obligation.

Unfortunately, the legitimate functions of the footnote are sometimes overshadowed by a teacher's obsessive concern with typographical style. There is a veritable tangle of different footnote and bibliography styles. The first problem is finding the style required for a particular paper. Once you find the one you need, use it correctly. The correct details about such matters are found in books or pamphlets called *style manuals*.

ON STYLE MANUALS

Primarily, style manuals set down—as if from on high—certain dos and don'ts that are of great concern to typesetters—how to punctuate a bibliography item, for instance, or how to use abbreviations in a footnote. The first style manuals were written in print shops, and many of them still are. It simply takes too much time—and money— to have typesetters argue about a question such as how much space goes after a period; so it is settled with an arbitrary rule. A style manual is a collection of arbitrary rules written down. It catalogs trivia and arbitrarily settles matters that are not worth arguing about.

When a teacher assigns a paper that will need documentation, he should tell you explicitly which style manual to follow. If he doesn't tell you, ask him. Sometimes he will not refer you to a manual, because no manual is standard in the field. He may refer you instead to a particular journal, for a number of professional journals include directions in the front of each issue about matters of typographical style. And those that don't will at least provide some models to follow.

If you expect to be writing much in a field where a standard style manual is available, you probably ought to buy your own copy. Below is a list of widely used manuals:

> Biological Sciences: *Style Manual for Biological Journals*. 2d ed. Washington, D.C.: American Institute of Biological Sciences, 1964.
> Chemistry: *Handbook for Authors*. Washington, D.C.: American Chemical Society, 1965.
> Engineering and related areas: George C. Harwell. *Technical Communication*. New York: Macmillan, 1960.
> History: Wood Gray *et al. Historian's Handbook*. Boston: Houghton Mifflin, 1964.
> Medicine: Morris Fishbein. *Medical Writing: The Technic and the Art*. 3rd ed. New York: McGraw-Hill, 1957.
> Modern languages, literature, and related fields: William R.

Parker. *The MLA Style Sheet.* New York: Modern Language Association, 1964.

Physics: *Style Manual.* New York: American Institute of Physics, 1959.

Psychology: *Publication Manual.* Washington, D.C.: American Psychological Association, 1967.

General: Kate L. Turabian. *A Manual for Writers of Term Papers, Theses, and Dissertations.* 3rd ed. Chicago: University of Chicago Press, 1967.

ON SERENDIPITY

Serendipity has been defined as "the fine art of stumbling onto something," but perhaps a better, at least more decorous, definition would be: a capacity to make fortunate and helpful discoveries by accident. Never underestimate serendipity. It is possible to discover some very interesting things when you least expect them, and when you do stumble across something, it is wise to look down and see what it is. Remember that Columbus stumbled across the New World on his way, he thought, to India.

Serendipity, like creativity, remains essentially a gift from the gods. But a writer can load the odds a bit in his favor. He can put his mind into a state where it is most likely to be visited with an inspiration, and he can also put himself into a position where he is most likely to be visited with serendipity. When a mind is filled with a subject and has been exercised enough so that it can move with quickness and precision, then it very likely will be able to detect connections between things that it might not have been able to connect in an intellectually lazier condition. You might, for instance, notice in passing the connection between a title on a library or bookstore shelf and your subject, even though neither the author of the book nor the person who cataloged and shelved it may have been thinking of any such connection. So after you have exhausted all the "standard" reference techniques, you can often find something very helpful by simply strolling through your library or local bookstore with an open eye.

Don't departmentalize your activities. Keep a number of different projects simmering all of the time (which is not too difficult in view of the typical class load), and then think and write about one in the language of another. Leaf through the indexes of some of your textbooks from other, unrelated classes. Don't think that the material learned for history class counts only for history, nor that what you learn from biological science counts only for science. Try to keep ideas reflecting one off the other.

Don't limit your search to the classroom. See what is coming in over the educational television channel or over the commercial channels, for some of their specials can be helpful. Ask around. You never can tell when you might stumble across somebody who knows something you don't. Listen to what the people around you talk about. It is surprising how often, if your mind is set for it, you find magazine articles and hear conversations that bear upon your problem. It doesn't always work that way, but when it does—that's serendipity. In short, court the magical abilities of the three princes of Serendip—all of whom had a truly remarkable ability for "falling into it."

NOTE

1. Richard D. Altick, *The Art of Literary Research* (New York: Norton, 1963), p. 171.

3 HOW TOOLS CAN HELP

It is always a pleasure to discover how much help a few simple tools can be. For instance, especially in longer, more complex writing projects, the simple job of keeping track of and manipulating the bits and pieces of paper can be frustrating and enervating. But a small investment in the right equipment can make the job of "moving the paper around" considerably easier: a straightedge (for tearing big pieces of paper into little ones), scissors (preferably eight or nine inches long), a three-hole punch, a stapler, a good staple remover, perhaps some rubber cement, a large roll of transparent tape (especially the kind you can write on), and a set of sturdy three-ring binders. You might even invest a modest sum in such miscellaneous things as carbon paper and a new typewriter ribbon. The former can be used as a safeguard against the loss of a theme by an instructor. The latter can be a particularly welcome courtesy to instructors who must read stacks of papers, more often than not under artificial light late at night.

ON PAPER

Modern paper comes in a multiplicity of guises and sizes. It can be as cheap and expendable as a

Kleenex or as expensive as the hand-crafted parchment used by certain Japanese artists. People who write a good deal know that drafting requires a lot of paper. They are prepared to draft and rewrite and draft again, so they are apt to use cheap paper for their early drafts. Yellow "second" sheets are good—not only are they cheaper than regular bond paper, but they can be distinguished by their color from finished copy. Newsprint is also a good drafting paper—and probably the cheapest of all.

Cheap paper offers certain psychological advantages in addition to thrift during early drafting. It reminds you that *this* is zero draft, not finished copy, and that you do not have much of an investment in it—either financial or emotional. Cheap paper can remind you to keep first things first. Using yellow sheets or rough-textured newsprint can be a bit of ritualization that encourages uninhibited drafting. The cheap paper is a reminder that you are not cutting words in marble slabs but are instead composing on disposable, cuttable paper—a medium uniquely open to change, revision, second and third thoughts.

A finished manuscript should be typed on 8½-by-11-inch white, standard, sixteen-pound bond paper. Good bond paper is much cheaper bought by the ream. The erasable bond, so popular with students, is hard to write on with a pencil or pen and tends to dissolve if it accidentally gets wet. But if you plan to use it, buy the twenty-pound weight to avoid irritating print-through from one page to the next. And never use onion skin: It is guaranteed to drive a reader blind faster than anything else. This concern over the paper for your finished copy is very practical, for you should want to turn in work that gives an immediate impression of quality.

THE LOOSE-LEAF BINDER SYSTEM

Advice about using cheap paper for drafting and quality paper for finished copy is simple enough, but that which follows is more complex, for it offers a procedure that anticipates the demands of editing—that important stage between initial drafts and finished copy. During editing, a draft is cut into pieces; the pieces are moved around, and insertions are made. Without some sort of systematic control over the cuts and insertions, editing can be a hectic and confusing job. The loose-leaf system offers just the kind of flexible control that can take the chaos out of editing.

The system requires two kinds of paper. First are the *backing sheets*—the cheapest 8½-by-11-inch, three-hole binder-filler you can find. If you try the system but have trouble finding inexpensive prepunched paper, you can turn cheap 8½-by-11-inch paper into backing sheets with a bit of time and a three-hole punch.

The system also requires *strips*—paper no more than 7½ inches wide—just narrow enough to be taped, glued, or stapled to the backing sheets without covering up the holes. You can use a scissors or a metal straightedge to trim regular-size paper to the proper width. Or you can buy a roll of shelf paper thirteen inches wide and, using a yardstick, tear it lengthwise into two strips and draft on that. Or you can buy strips from a local printer who can cut them out of a large stock into pieces that are about 7½ inches wide and 17 inches long.

The extra length of the strips is just an accident, but it has certain advantages. It can encourage you to keep drafting once you start a page until you write at least 500 words, and it means less fiddling with the typewriter, less changing paper, and so forth. Eric Berne, the author of *Games People Play,* used something like the ultimate system: he mounted a roll of paper over his typewriter and drafted on one long, continuous strip, a certain number of yards per session.

With the binder system, you draft on the strips, cut or tear the strips into convenient, more or less unified pieces, fasten them to the backing sheets, and then file everything in a loose-leaf binder. Stapling is probably the best way to attach the strips to the backing sheets. It is fast and handy, and a good staple remover allows you to cut up pieces of draft and move them from one backing sheet to another with relative ease. Also, if you use a stapler and a good staple remover, the same backing sheet can be used again and again, although in time the margins may become so heavily marked up that the sensibilities of even the most casual of writers might be offended.

The binder system is especially helpful for those who have a pack-rat attitude toward gathering material for a writing job—and toward study in general. Since many good ideas have been lost that a quick note might have saved, a pack-rat attitude is a very desirable thing. In his book *The Art of Thinking,* Ernest Dimnet advised: "The moment we realize that any thought, ours or borrowed, is pregnant enough not to be wasted or original enough not to be likely to come

FIGURE 2. A page from a zero draft that has received some editing. The copy is written on narrow *strip* paper (or in some cases, just scraps) and stapled to plain binder-filler, or *backing sheets,* leaving plenty of white space for editorial notes. Notice that only one side of each backing sheet is used.

back again, we must fix it on paper." [1] The binder system encourages the capture of fugitive ideas, and it provides a handy way to keep track of them once they are caught. In fact, the binder system can be used as a filing system that is no less effective (and for students in many ways more convenient) than the much more expensive filing system that uses Manila folders and big metal cabinets.

With a ninety-eight-cent three-hole punch, a stapler, scissors, backing paper, and a set of binders, you can preserve any stray note of whatever size or shape. Dittoed handouts, lecture notes, term papers, and old examinations can be punched and put in place. Oversize material can be folded and cut and then stapled to backing sheets. Maps and charts, clippings and magazine articles can be slipped into envelopes that have been taped to backing sheets. One important thing to remember, however, is that a filing system is only useful if it is partially empty. You must have space to put new material. You should keep a stock of more binders and backing sheets than you immediately need.

One other advantage of the binder system is that, because it handles bits and pieces easily and allows a sort of controlled messiness, it encourages getting ideas down on paper—no matter how primitively. Students very often say that they cannot sit down and start writing until they have things set fairly well in their minds, and this belief more often than not undermines their writing efforts. Jean Guitton, in *A Student's Guide to Intellectual Work,* emphasizes the advantage of "forcing yourselves to write the thing down . . . for better or for worse, unhesitatingly, irrevocably":

> You would not believe what an advantage it is to have this initial resistant material to which you can apply yourself. . . . *The most deplorable sentence is better than a blank sheet of paper.* . . . The thing to do is to pick up your raw material and get your hands dirty.[2]

Some writers, admittedly, do much or all of their zero drafting in their heads. Such a procedure is fine—if there is time, and if you are sure that you are not using the drafting-in-the-head ploy to avoid the uncomfortable job of getting started at the real writing.

The person who can draft in his head is usually someone who works on writing full time or at least is involved with his material full time. But with the American college's cut-up, piecemeal curriculum, students are always part-time writers at best, and part-time writers have to be able to drop their writing and pick it up again later. Drafting on paper fits the part-time situation much better than does trying to keep the work completely inside you, and the binder system makes part-time drafting manageable. With its ability to accumulate and to cope with bits and pieces as well as extended stretches of prose, the system reminds the part-time writer that he doesn't have to do the job all at once and that he does not have to draft in any special order. He can let the ideas come as they will and sort them at his leisure.

Cutting strips of draft into pieces for mounting on backing sheets may seem to be a simple mechanical task, but it is really the first big step toward editing. Accordingly, there is more detailed advice about sorting and mounting in Chapter 8, pages 97–99. Students who like to have the phases of drafting and editing separated by as much time as possible let the strips pile up, delaying any kind of editing until they are finished with early drafting. Other students cut the strips and mount the pieces after each drafting session, preferring to review each day's work as they go along. In either case, the purpose is that of any filing system: to keep closely related material together.

The basic idea of the binder system is to enable you to cope with fugitive ideas, however briefly expressed, as well as with longer pieces of sustained draft. Sometimes in the course of a writing project enough bits of fugitive ideas are filed together to form a packet of sustained prose. At other times, and perhaps more commonly, reading back through these fugitive bits can give you hints and suggestions that can inspire longer spurts of drafting. In either case, one of the advantages of the binder system is that it helps you spot and keep track of these fugitive ideas, no matter what their editorial fate.

Perhaps every writer has experienced, at least once, the luck of inspiration, when an entire piece flowed out in one single, coherent stream without a hitch or a halt. Although good writers know how to edit to make it look as if writing always happens that way, most of the time it does not. A realistic view of drafting includes not only those stretches of sustained prose, but also sketches, experiments, notes, piecemeal work, jottings, queries, comments on sources—in short, all sorts of "backup." And the binder system encourages the habit of accumulation and the virtue of persistence, which so often are the precursors of inspiration.

GETTING THE WORDS ON PAPER

So far as the actual method of setting down draft is concerned, typing rather than writing in longhand seems preferable. Typing is more efficient, faster, and encourages a standardized format for early drafts and notes: standard-size paper, generous margins, double- or triple-spaced lines, use of only one side of paper. All of these are very desirable habits to develop. Of course, if using a typewriter clashes with personal idiosyncrasy, it is probably better to forgo the efficiency and to write in longhand. But no matter what writing method is used, employing a standardized format should become a habit.

Those who prefer writing in longhand have an incredible array of pen types to choose among, but the lowly pencil has its advocates, too. Some people—sometimes people who write a great deal—prefer the pencil for all stages of their writing. A number-two pencil, or its equivalent, appears to have about the right degree of hardness.

Other helpful tools include black felt markers and felt highlighting pens. The highlighting pens with transparent ink can be helpful, since various colors can be used for marking words and passages so as to call attention to them without covering the type or print on the page. Black felt markers are good for crossing out material during the editing stages.

USING A TAPE RECORDER

Many students are intrigued with the possibilities of using tape recorders or dictating machines for their early drafting. Dictating is not an uncommon way to draft. Earle Stanley Gardner, prolific author of the Perry Mason mystery novels, dictated his books, as did Henry James and the blind John Milton. The method is not unique to the writers of fiction or epics, however, for the great historian Francis Parkman dictated *The Oregon Trail*.

The most obvious advantage of dictation is that it is fast. Once a writer gets used to the machine itself, he can talk to it much faster than he can push a pencil or the keys of a typewriter and thus can more easily save those good, but unfortunately will-of-the-wisp, ideas that might otherwise have been lost.

Some people find that, although they can speak well in conversation, they have trouble when they sit down to draft. A tape recorder can be indispensable to such people, for all they have to do is line up a willing listener, turn on the recorder, and start "talking" their zero draft. If the listener interrupts, so much the better; a sense of dialogue can help the writer a great deal. Later, it is fairly easy to sit at the typewriter and draft from a tape as long as the tape is used as a stimulant to drafting—rather than a substitute for it. If you use this conversational technique, remember that you don't have to make an exact transcript of the tape recording. Very often in conversation ideas are not expressed very well. The tape machine offers a rare opportunity to go back over a conversation and say all of the things you later wish you had said—that witty retort, that devastating criticism thought of too late—can be put down later while drafting. With this technique you are like a dramatist who writes conversation the way it should have been, rather than the way it was.

If you choose the more standard, less conversational approach to zero drafting with a tape recorder, it might be well to try an exercise such as the following to familiarize yourself with the machine and the techniques of dictation. After reading an essay or a chapter from a textbook or listening to a lecture, try to reconstruct the contents without looking at the written text or consulting any notes. Dictate into the machine what you believe was said, including any reactions and questions. Later, use your lecture notes or the text itself to check on your accuracy. Reconstructing lectures, chapters, and essays is a good study technique as well as good practice in drafting.

Not looking at notes during the dictation exercise forces you to hold in mind the overall shape of an argument, its direction, and your relative position in it—an important ability to have when drafting on tape rather than on paper. If you are tempted to use many redundant words and phrases, give in to the temptation; such redundancies can help keep track of where you are in the argument. Later, what is unnecessary can be marked out. Some redundancies are repetitions of an idea, and the second or third expression of it may be better than the first. When editing, you can keep only the best.

If nothing else, the dictation exercise should help you grow more adept with the mechanical operation of the machine itself. The exercise also should help you overcome that sense of self-consciousness and embarrassment that most people feel when they encounter a dictating machine. For reasons not altogether clear, a dictating machine can be an intimidating instrument.

A tape recorder can be handy to the writer for things other than drafting. For instance, reading the entire draft aloud and then listening to the playback often calls attention to blunders that might otherwise be missed. A tape recorder can also be used to record lectures, interviews, conferences, discussions, radio programs, even the audio from television programs.

When buying a tape recorder for dictation, there are certain features to look for. A portable machine is best, preferably one that is transistorized and has a stop-and-start switch on the microphone. An automatic volume control to compensate for differences in volume is a particularly helpful feature for recording discussions, although it makes the machine less desirable for recording music. It is possible to buy a good machine with these features for around fifty dollars.

The following anecdote illustrates a number of the pitfalls and advantages of the tape recorder: One student, an avid devotee of electronic gadgets, decided to get part of his zero draft by tape-recording an interview with a professor of psychology. He had prepared a set of questions on perceptual psychology and had a clear opinion about the issue, so he was set for the interview. He brought in his tape recorder, plugged it in, and spent nearly an hour in deep conversation with the professor. The whole affair became an intense session of learning. The student came away from the conference elated, until he unpacked the recorder in his room and discovered that he had pushed the wrong button and that there was nothing on the tape. Faced with a blank tape, he sat down and reconstructed the dialogue from memory. In doing so, he gave the conversation a coherence and a force that most likely were not in the original. The mechanism of recording had freed him for a full human involvement that allowed him to discard the irrelevancies and to remember the essentials of the conversation. He said afterward that although he would use the machine again, he would not attempt to work from the tape of an interview; rather, he would sit down and attempt to reconstruct it. The tape would remain something to resort to when necessary and only after the reconstruction had been finished. We recommend the same technique for all such uses of the recorder—along with remembering to push the right button.

BOOKS ABOUT WORDS

Every college student should have a good desk dictionary—not a paperback, but one of those volumes that weighs at least three or four pounds. There are six truly first-rate, college-level desk dictionaries to choose from. Listed chronologically, they are:

1. *The American Heritage Dictionary of the English Language.* Boston and New York: American Heritage and Houghton Mifflin, 1969.
2. *The Random House Dictionary of the English Language: College Edition.* New York: Random House, 1968, which is based on *The Random House Dictionary of the English Language: Unabridged Edition.* New York: Random House, 1966.

3. *Funk and Wagnalls Standard College Dictionary: Text Edition.* New York: Harcourt, Brace & World, 1964.
4. *Webster's Seventh New Collegiate Dictionary.* Springfield, Mass.: G. & C. Merriam, 1963, which is based on *Webster's Third New International Dictionary.* Springfield, Mass.: G. & C. Merriam, 1961.
5. *Webster's New World Dictionary of the American Language.* Cleveland, Ohio: World Publishing, 1953.
6. *The American College Dictionary.* New York: Random House, 1947.

Since one dictionary tends, by the nature of things, to learn from those published before it, and since the English language is constantly changing, the most recent dictionaries are in general the most desirable. But there are some differences among the six, so that not all are equally adaptable to particular tastes and needs. For instance, etymological information can be very helpful to the writer, as we shall discuss further in Chapter 7. In general, *The Random House Dictionary* and *The American Heritage Dictionary* seem to have fuller etymologies than the other three. The *New Collegiate Dictionary* seems to be particularly strong in technical and scientific material. Still, in total coverage and price, the dictionaries tend to be very much alike. All six are so good that you would not do badly in choosing any of them. Just be sure to get one of these six. And if you are a truly serious user of the language, get two, so that you can play one off against the other. One general warning: The people who write the blurbs for the dust jackets of dictionaries are fond of the word "authoritative," but do not trust that word. There is no truly authoritative dictionary of the English language, simply because no dictionary can include everything, and because the language keeps changing all the time.

One further suggestion: Some of the most informative, most carefully written essays on dictionaries and their uses are in the fronts of dictionaries. These valuable essays are too often left unread. Read them, for time spent with that front matter is time well spent.

Finally, for more etymological information than that provided in a desk dictionary, the very best etymological source—available in most public and school libraries—is the twelve-volume *Oxford English Dictionary,* a work that you should get to know. When consulting the *OED,* be sure to check the supplement at the end. There are also a number of less expensive etymological dictionaries, should you be interested in getting one for your private reference collection. Among them are C. T. Onions' *The Oxford Dictionary of English Etymology* (Oxford, Eng.: Oxford University Press, 1966) and Eric Partridge's *Origins: A Short Etymological Dictionary of Modern English* (New York: Macmillan, 1959). If you are a genuine word hound, you might spend some time exploring the reference section of your library, where there are dictionaries you never dreamed existed, some of which, if not too helpful, are at least extremely interesting.

Roget's *Thesaurus* is probably the single most popular reference book among student writers. Unfortunately, although a thesaurus can foster good style, used ineptly it can destroy it. A thesaurus should not be used as a treasure store for new words. If a writer uses it as if it were, he might use words he does not know well enough to apply accurately and fittingly. A thesaurus serves best when it is used simply to recall words already known and familiar but momentarily forgotten. If at any time you should take a new word from a thesaurus, look the word up in a regular dictionary, carefully paying attention to any competing synonyms. For more detailed—and often more helpful—treatment of synonyms than is provided in desk dictionaries, *Webster's Dictionary of Synonyms,* 2d ed. (Springfield, Mass.: G. & C. Merriam, 1968) lists synonyms and provides careful discriminations among the meanings of closely related words. It also lists antonyms and analogous and contrasted words. It would make a useful supplement to your regular desk dictionary—if only to help restrain hasty and uncontrolled use of Roget's work.

NOTES

1. Ernest Dimnet, *The Art of Thinking* (Greenwich, Conn.: Fawcett, 1961), p. 157.
2. Jean Guitton, *A Student's Guide to Intellectual Work,* trans. Adrienne Foulke Notre Dame, Ind.: University of Notre Dame Press, 1965), p. 54.

CONTEMPLATION: IMAGES AND TONES 4

Prose that is concrete gives the reader a sense of touching life directly. In such prose a topic is not under glass in a specimen case, nor is it held abstractly high with philosophical purity. It is nose-close, within rubbing distance—with no glass, no philosophy between it and the writer or his reader. To write concrete prose one must use words that evoke images. To get those words that evoke images a writer must first sensuously feel what he writes about as if he were in touch with it, seeing it, smelling it at that very moment of drafting. To do that literally is impossible—or nearly so. One can't harpoon a white whale from a small boat and simultaneously draft about it. What the writer must do is use the power he has to see things with his eyes closed. He must use his "third eye," his power to blend abstract concepts with sensuous memories to create mental images. To get the imagery he needs a writer lets his mind's eye contemplate a scene (remembered or imagined) that embodies his theme.

Contemplation of a scene can move the writer's mind, for instance, from abstractions about capital punishment to details about the act of execution such as the petroleum jelly, the spots of shaven skin, and the thick straps of an electric chair at the end of death row. Contemplation can move the writer from an abstraction such as "the deleterious effects of rural poverty" past the plodding lethargy of the chronically underfed, to a scene within a tenant farmer's cabin and to the dried scabs and the sharp stench of a neglected child. It can move him from "the solitary beauties of the Oregon coast" to the fragile trail the bare feet of a lone girl leave on tide-smoothed sand.

To demonstrate the power of a scene evoked especially for the sake of contemplation, consider the technique of one who is engaged in religious meditation—upon, say, Christ's mercy and love. He calls up as vividly as possible a scene such as that of Christ's crucifixion. He visualizes the scene of the three crosses. He tries to call up details: the line of the hill against the lowering sky, the nervous joking of the soldiers, the smell of the crowd, the deep brown stain of dried blood —in short, the total array of sensations. He does so to focus his attention so as to achieve a concrete, sensuous link between himself and the object of his meditation. This link helps him approach the issue of Christ's mercy and love not only intellectually but also emotionally; it clarifies and reaffirms his emotional stance.

The choice of scene can help focus one's treatment of a subject. For instance, writing based on the scene at Calvary would treat Christ's love in one way; writing based on the scene with the adulteress would treat it in quite a different way; writing based on the Last Supper scene would treat it in even another. Different scenes heighten different attributes and thus focus and limit one's treatment of a subject. The secret is to try out different scenes as a means to understand the abstractions and generalities of the subject matter, and then to choose the scene that seems to produce the desired stance.

The following is a scene from a student's paper, a scene that is used to make more tangible the self-discipline and dedication necessary to a successful athlete. The scene is somewhat "staged." Though drawn from the writer's experiences, the description of the lone basketball player is idealized in a way that suggests clearly that he was invented to represent a certain type—the dedicated, disciplined athlete:

> The self-discipline that patience brings is of great importance if an individual is to learn the value of practice. Practice enhances an athlete's ability to produce when called upon, to come through under pressure. Practice is not easy; it is tedious, exhausting

work that demands intense concentration and total dedication to purpose. Practice is also aloneness. It is jogging in the early morning while the rest of the world sleeps. It is the athlete who remains to improve skills after everyone else has gone home:

> The gymnasium is empty except for some crumpled programs and dried-up apple cores. All the lights are out except the one at the far end of the building. From that direction a steady plodding of solitary feet can be heard. A ball thuds sporadically against the floor, interrupted by the occasional swishing sound of a basketball ripping through the nylon corded netting of a basket. A lone figure cuts through the key and fakes against an imaginary opponent. The pattern continues, far-reaching, merging with the silence of the night.

IMAGES AND SCENES

Contemplation is a mode of thought based upon the following psychological chain of events:

Experience comes originally in the form of sensations; it is retained by the mind in the form of images. Tastes, sights, sounds, smells—these are sensations. A sensation represents a particular physical, external event, whereas an image is a mental re-creation of a sensation. Thus, a person can have visual sensations only if his eyes are open, but he can have visual images when his eyes are closed. Though experience is stored in the mind as images, only some images record the sensations of one's own experience, whereas others record someone else's report of his experience. Images of the first kind—which we can call *direct*—are those that are based on the direct recording of one's own sensations—tastes, sights, sounds, smells. Direct images are mental re-creations of such sensations. Images of the second kind—which we can call *vicarious*—are those that are based on someone else's report of his sensations. Vicarious images are only indirectly based on one's own sensations.

For instance, when someone eats a meal, he experiences a number of sensations—basically, the sensations of eating, which are tastes, smells, textures, sights, and even sounds. But if he reads a concrete description of a meal, the direct sensations he gets are those of reading, not of eating. The images that he is likely to retain—if the writing is good—are very similar to those he would have retained had he actually eaten the meal. Thus, the experiences out of which images are derived need not be direct; they can be vicarious. A vicarious experience comes from one's source material—historical or fictional, a story told by a friend or an episode described in books on behavioral or social science.

Vicarious images are possible because, though direct images are originally bound to particular personal experiences, they can be freed from their private origins and recomposed into new arrangements. It is this loosening of direct images from the bonds of solely private, personal experience that allows vicarious images to be built out of parts and pieces of old direct imagery. Ultimately, though, reported or not, any experience stored in the mind as an image was originally grounded through sensations to a particular time and place, a particular scene, something that happened to someone. At their point of origin, images are bound to a scene vividly experienced as if existing here and now, which is why the writer must revert to a scene to retap the basic imagery latent in a subject.

ON MAKING A SCENE

Close the books. Shut your eyes and loosen your mind's images with meditation. Within your mind evoke a scene that embodies your subject. Ponder its detail. Trace its emotion. Then by writing a description of that scene, you will begin to find the concrete words that will help infuse your writing with a personal, direct impact and tone. This will better enable you to write prose in which things still have feelings stuck to them, in which things are still somehow all mixed up with what people are and do and feel.

When a scene is imagined, the one imagining it is mentally viewing it from some one place. For most purposes the natural place to start with seems to be somewhat outside and a bit above the scene—as if viewing a stage play from a balcony seat. Balcony distance is good because at first you must be able to attend to the larger details of the scene.

When a writer describes a scene as if he knew all that could be known about the scene, including the characters' thoughts and feelings, his point of view is *omniscient*. When he limits himself to the outward appearances of the scene, his point of view is *dramatic*. As a start toward gathering details from a scene, the dramatic point of view is best. It keeps the mind focused on the things and the appearances of things; it keeps the mind focused on the stuff out of which images are made.

Once you have found a scene for your subject, your first description of it should be from slightly above and outside the frame of the scene as you imagine it. Find the psychological center of the scene first. In the crucifixion example, Christ's cross would be the psychological center for most contemplations of it. Once the center is fixed, stage the scene as a dramatist would. Make a drawing—not necessarily detailed, just a quick crude sketch of who and what your imagination has put into the scene. Then start writing. Remember that this first description is not expected to be finished prose. It is zero draft and in this case might at first be little more than a simple list.

As you write your description, move from the center to the left, then from the center to the right, then fill in the background. At balcony distance the senses of sight and sound—and thus visual and aural images—will dominate most scenes. So describe what your mind can see first—the shapes, the heights, the widths of things; then the colors and angles, the shadows, and the relationships to the central figure. Then describe what your mind can hear: What sounds are there? Where do they come from?

To bring *all* of the senses into play, you must move closer, out of the balcony seat and into the scene itself. But even though you are closer to the people in the scene now, your point of view is still dramatic and you should still treat them simply as other things. Stay outside their skins and minds for the time being. Moving the mind over the scene in the same way as before, notice thing after thing. As you notice each thing, take the time to notice it sense by sense. Carefully disengage each sense in the imagination before moving on to the next. The imagination recalls past sensations and images best if you limit its focus—rather the way a serious kiss feels better if you close your eyes, and the way it feels better to have somebody *else* scratch your back. When *you* do it, the sensations of moving your arm and fingers cancel out the sensuous pleasures of an itch being scratched.

Figure 3 charts the kinds of questions that can be asked—using all of the senses. Not all of the questions can be applied each time, but you should try each one. At first you may need the list to remind you

QUESTIONING THE SENSES

Seeing It

What *position* is it in?
> How far is it from you? How far is it from the central figure of the scene? in what direction? What is beside it? above it? below it? in front of it? behind it?

What *shape* is it?
> Is it mostly angles, or is it mostly curves? Are there many small angles or curves, or are there just a few large ones? Is it flat, or does it give a sense of depth? What else is that shape?

What *size* is it?
> Is it large or small compared with you? Is it large or small compared with the central figure of the scene? What else is that size?

What *color* is it?
> Which color seems to dominate? Do the colors contrast sharply, or do they merge? Are they bright, or are they shadowed? Where is the light coming from? What sort of light is it? What else is that color?

Is it *moving*?
> If so, is all of it moving, or just certain parts? Is the movement abrupt? rapid? slow? fluttering? fluid? What else moves like that?

Hearing It

Is there sound in the scene? Is there just one sound, or are there many? What sort of sound is dominant? Is it like music, or is it like noise? Is it rhythmic or random? Is it soft or loud? Is it high in pitch or low? Is it constant or changing? If there is any background sound, what sort of sound is it? What else sounds like the sounds of this scene?

Touching It

If you touched it, would it be cold or warm? would it be wet or dry? would it feel oily? would it feel slick but not oily? How soft would it be? how hard? Would it be smooth, or would it be rough? Would the surface flake? Would it scratch? Would it respond at all? What else feels like that?

Smelling It

Is there just one smell, or are there many? How strong is the dominant smell? Does it smell like flowers? Is it like fruit? like spice? Is it a burned smell? a resinous smell? putrid? How would you characterize the background smells? What else smells like the smells of this scene?

Tasting It

If you tasted the thing, would it be sweet? Would it be salty? sour? bitter? How strong would the taste be? Would it be mixed? What else tastes that way?

FIGURE 3.

of all the ways your body senses things; learning to contemplate means learning to remember all the ways your body comes in contact with things. Soon you will need no such list.

The last senses you can call upon when describing your scene are those that only you can receive, because they are completely inside you. Describe how you feel about each separate detail of the scene you have just seen and heard, felt, tasted, and smelled. Ask yourself, "Did this detail disturb me or comfort me? Was it pleasant or painful, or was it just there, a neuter?"

If all of this emphasis on contemplation and the knowledge contained in the sensations of the body seems insufficiently "goal-oriented," you might consider the following ancient Chinese poem quoted by Alan Watts in his book *The Way of Zen:*

> Sitting quietly, doing nothing,
> Spring comes, and the grass grows by itself.

Watts speaks further of "the mind's and the world's natural way of action . . . when the eyes see by themselves and the ears hear by themselves, and the mouth opens by itself without having to be forced apart by the fingers." [1]

EMPATHY AND TONE

The hallmark of most good writing of any kind is the clear sense in the reader that the writer knows how he feels about his subject, that he is committed and prepared to admit his commitment, that he has a distinct emotional stance toward his subject and has found a voice for that stance.

One way to explore your feelings toward a subject is to contemplate and describe a scene as discussed in the preceding sections. To discover and stabilize your emotional stance, you should imagine what it would be like to be in that scene. When imagining the scene, ask, "What would it feel like to be that person? or *that* one?" "With which person in the scene do I identify?" "Where in the scene would I put myself?"

Notice the progression: from abstraction (for instance, Christ's mercy and love) to a scene that dramatizes those abstractions (such as Calvary) to the contemplation of the intense and detailed imagery of the scene (for example, the blood, the cries, the dark sky) to an empathic identification with one of the characters of the scene. From abstraction to image to empathy—such is one sequence that leads to a distinct stance and a controlled voice.

The following example is part of a student's zero draft written for a paper dealing with the problems of teaching English to children in the ghetto. In the example she attempts to empathize with one of the black children:

> I'm sittin on the floor doin my English. My ma tell me to get up and stop the toilet from runnin. I'm countin them same cracks in the wall. The air sure blows through um. Maybe ma will let me sleep in my winter coat tonight. Today my English teacher learned us a lot bout the way we sposed to talk. Most time we don't talk much to each other at my house, but for some reason it's always noisy there. The baby cryin and people yellin at everybody else. Grampa yells too. He can't hear the t.v. so he turns it up real loud. I plug my ears when I do my homework. The floor is cold to my seat, but there no place else to sit. And I want to learn them new words so I can pass the test like I'm sposed to. I do better in rithmetic than English.

Using empathy is a particularly helpful technique when dealing with a subject that involves people in action and thus has a certain dramatic potential, such as history, literature, sociology, anthropology, or psychology. When imagining a scene dealing with a subject such as civil rights or suicide remember that no two people would cope with the situation in the same way—nor would they have the same stances.

The way that different stances can be acknowledged and explored is illustrated nicely through the adventures of one student who was writing a paper on the moral issues involved in heart transplants. She tried first to call up a scene in which she would empathize with a white man in South Africa who had been given the heart of a black man. It didn't work. She then tried to empathize with a sick person whose heart was failing and who could be saved with a transplant. Again she drew an emotional blank. She then tried to empathize with a surgeon who had to decide which of two dying patients would receive the one heart available for transplant—a dilemma borrowed from a television drama that was broadcast while she was working on her paper. Again, she found it impossible to make the empathic leap. Finally, she tried to empathize with a seriously injured woman entering a hospital where she knows a transplant team is waiting for a donor's heart. This scene worked. She had found her emotional stance.

The process of imaginative scene-making and empathizing can help a writer mark his prose with a personal tone. He doesn't even need a written description of the scene in his final draft, for the tone may be set by little more than a handful of verbs and adjectives that the scene inspired—not much perhaps, but those words, all based on a single scene, can breathe into a page of prose a unique, recognizable human voice.

The tones conveyed in writing reflect the author's stance toward his subject. They reflect the quality of his involvement with it. Tone is conveyed in complex ways—in how a writer emphasizes some details and subordinates others, in the kinds of things he chooses not to say as well as the words he actually uses. The control of tone is a complicated problem, one of the most demanding and sophisticated in writing. But usually lapses in tone arise from images that contradict a writer's emotional stance. A good rule of thumb for maintaining control over tone is this: With a basic scene firmly in mind, with your role in that scene carefully chosen, and with your stance toward the subject well established, do not include any word or detail that contradicts the quality of that scene or the quality of the empathy attained.

NOTE

1. Alan Watts, *The Way of Zen* (New York: New American Library, 1959), p. 133.

5
HOW TO BE PRECISE

When material stubbornly remains general and its language lacks precision, a procedure to help control ideas and terms is needed. The procedure discussed in this chapter analyzes complex items into their attributes, and then uses the attributes as a basis for classification. It is a version of that kind of thinking described by the German philosopher Immanuel Kant when he said that

> . . . a great, perhaps the greatest, part of the business of our reason consists in analysis of the concepts which we already have of objects. This analysis supplies us with a considerable body of knowledge, which, while nothing but explanation or elucidation of what has already been thought in our concepts, though in a confused manner, is yet prized as being, at least as regards its form, new insight. But so far as the matter or content is concerned, there has been no extension of our previously possessed concepts, but only an analysis of them.[1]

This process of analyzing and classifying can make ideas more precise and can give a writer more things to say about his topic. It fixes a subject in his mind in order to encourage him to ask precise questions. Technically the procedure discussed in this chapter is known as *componential analysis,* but a student once dubbed it the "Idea Machine," which seems a somewhat more comfortable title.[2]

The Idea Machine's power as a drafting tool arises from the fact that your mind has stored away in that intricate filing system we call language much more thinking and observation about a given subject than you might imagine—even a subject about which you might feel you know very little. The Idea Machine is designed to help you analyze this filing system—to expose it so that you might see some things freshly, so that you might see better just how much you do in fact know about your subject and might better bring this unconscious knowledge into organized, controlled consciousness.

CATEGORIES AND ATTRIBUTES

One's vocabulary is a catalog of words with their conventional meanings. Words are names for concepts, not for individual things. Concepts are basically ways of categorizing individual things. When a word is used to name something, that thing is put into a category along with similar things with the same name. A category can be defined by listing the attributes that, taken together, determine whether or not a certain individual thing qualifies as a member of that category.

For instance, that concept named with the word "chair" makes it possible to place many superficially different things into the same category—that is, to give them the same name. It makes no difference that they might vary one from the other a great deal: Some will have a straight back, some will be curved and padded; some will have arms, some will not; some will have four legs, some perhaps three, some only one; some will be those great ugly things you sit in to get your teeth fixed, some will be the pretty, fragile things that stand before a lady's vanity. But we overlook these many differences in order to register the similar attributes that they have and to say, finally, "All of these things, different as they might seem to be on the surface, share certain crucial attributes and thus belong to the same category. All are covered by the same concept, which we label 'chair.' "

The crucial attributes for a chair would appear to be such things as the following: that it is designed to sit in; that it is designed to hold one person; that the distance from the top of the seat to the floor or the footrest is roughly that of the distance from the knee to the sole; that the item has a back. These attributes are crucial, because anything that does not have them does not qualify for that category "chair." Noncrucial attributes would be such things as the color of the item, the number of legs, the presence of arms, the kind of material with which it is covered. Noncrucial attributes do not affect whether or not the item is categorized as a chair; they represent an area of allowable variation within the category.

Thus, when someone says something like, "That is a chair," he is not just pointing to a given thing in a given time and place and hanging a label on it. He is categorizing that thing, controlling it with a concept that includes all of the chairs in the world and excludes all of the non-chairs. He is categorizing that item in a way that heightens the crucial attributes and mutes the noncrucial ones.

Everything in the world can be sorted into simple categories on the basis of the presence or absence of just one attribute. One attribute produces two categories, because a thing either has the attribute or it does not. Thus all of the things in the world can be divided into groups, such as, for instance, those things that are pink versus those things that are not pink. Again, any one attribute produces two categories: the category made up of those things that share the attribute and the category made up of those things that do not.

Normally all one notices of the incredibly complicated network of attributes and categories in his language is that small part needed at the moment. But the complex classification systems are there, in one's mind, directing his perceptions of the world. The Idea Machine is a device for analyzing into their attributes the concepts labeled with words.

Though the Idea Machine works equally well with source material, we will use a passage from a student's zero draft to show how it can help expand and control the unruly ideas in early draft:

> Here in this country of ours we preach that a man ought to be free. Surely a man ought to be free to decide whether he wants to live or die. A man should not be free to decide whether or not somebody else should be able to live or die, but he should be able to decide about himself. What if he is feeling great physical pain, and there is no hope for a cure? And emotional pain can

be just as awful. Murder is wrong, but suicide isn't murder. And yet society says that suicide is wrong. We kill enemy soldiers in a war. Society says that one man has the right to decide about another there, why not with suicide? What about executions? Suicide should not be treated by society as a crime.

Clearly, the writer of this passage is much involved with some complicated problems of definition. Basically, he is dealing with one type of killing — suicide — that is currently defined by society as illegal and socially unacceptable, and he would like to have at least that part of the definition changed. It would be helpful for him to clearly define various kinds of killing, which would be rather complicated, since the English language provides a number of different terms to denote carefully distinguished kinds of killing.

In cases like this the "brainstorming" method that is favored by some management groups is helpful to start the Idea Machine. In a brainstorming session one just sits down, either alone or with one or two or more friends, and starts jotting down ideas as fast as they come. It is important to keep moving—for the momentum helps keep the new thoughts coming. It is important not to waste time quibbling and criticizing, but rather to get the ideas down as fast as possible. For example, in listing "Kinds of Killing," a brainstorming session might produce something like this:

suicide	hanging
murder	execution
natural death	war
cancer	religious sacrifice
cigarettes	homicide
butchering	auto accident
abortion	euthanasia
hunting	contraception
bullfighting	

The next step in the operation of the Idea Machine is to stop and try to sort things out, looking over the list and trying to find points of similarity and difference among the items on it. The secret is to look for attributes that are shared or not shared by various items on the list, as in the following:

Some of the terms (murder, hunting, execution, and so forth) seem to refer to kinds of killing that more or less parallel suicide.

Other kinds (natural death) do not seem to belong to that parallel series. Question: What are the crucial attributes here? The tentative answer might be that suicide and the others imply a human agent, a killer; natural death does not.

Other kinds (cancer) are not part of that parallel series, not only because they do not imply a human agent, but also because they are not kinds of killings as much as they are causes of death.

Some kinds of killing are obviously acceptable by our society (butchering, hunting, execution, war); others are definitely unacceptable (suicide, murder, religious sacrifice).

On the basis of a preliminary examination such as this, certain of the original items can be eliminated. A revised list might be something like this:

suicide	execution
murder	killing in war
butchering	religious sacrifice
abortion	accidental homicide
hunting	justifiable homicide
bullfighting	euthanasia

To keep the Idea Machine going, at least two attributes that can handily sort the items into different categories need to be spotted. There is usually one attribute that will come to mind quickly. The preceding list might immediately suggest the attribute of "social acceptability": Some kinds of killing are socially acceptable and others are not.

Don't hesitate to start with an obvious, immediately evident attribute, even though it may seem to produce a set of trivial categories. Some students draw a blank on their first try with these procedures because they believe they should come up with some grand scheme, some stunningly brilliant categorization. Remember the Ninth Rule of Descartes:

We ought to give the whole of our attention to the most insignificant and most easily mastered facts, and remain a long time in contemplation of them until we are accustomed to behold the truth clearly and distinctly.[3]

To focus the mind on its job of abstracting attributes from a list, one might use a series of questions: By whom was this done? for what? with what? when? under what circumstances? Who or what is affected? in what way? For example, asking the question "Who or what is affected by the killings?" might suggest a second attribute—the presence of a human victim.

The two attributes—social acceptability and the humanness of the victim—can be arranged in chart fashion to form a four-cell matrix upon which all of the items from the list can be placed (see Figure 4).

KINDS OF KILLING

	Human Victims	Nonhuman Victims
Socially Acceptable	execution war jusifiable homicide	butchering hunting
Socially Unacceptable	suicide murder abortion (?) religious sacrifice$_1$ accidental homicide euthanasia (?)	abortion (?) bullfighting religious sacrifice$_2$

FIGURE 4. A four-cell matrix that sorts kinds of killing on the basis of two attributes. The subscripts indicate different kinds of religious sacrifice. The question marks indicate some indecision about the victim in abortion and about the social acceptability of abortion and euthanasia.

Even this simple analysis raises certain rather precise questions: If abortion is taken as a form of killing, is the victim human or not? Are abortion and euthanasia really unacceptable in our country? The American public seems to be becoming, if not more liberal, at least more mixed in its attitude toward the woman who seeks abortion or the child who puts his hopeless and pain-ridden mother out of her misery. This trend, if there in fact is one, might be very relevant to a paper that attempts to argue for a similar liberalizing of our attitudes toward suicide. Abortion and euthanasia might well be areas that deserve additional thought and reading.

There is an important moral in this last observation: Notice that the "renegade" items, those that were troublesome when the Idea Machine was applied to them, raised the most fruitful questions. Always watch for the "misfit," and most certainly do not sweep it under the rug. The attempt to determine exactly why one element does not fit and the attempt to make it fit will very often push the mind into new areas of thought and produce new draft.

But this initial analysis is obviously not precise enough, for each category has too many different kinds of killing contained in it. We need to find at least one more attribute to increase our precision. The question, "What third attribute should be used?" can be devilishly difficult, and the attempt to answer it sometimes provides more insight and draft than does the answer itself. One fairly sensible way to start to find it would be to look for a specific feature that would contrast certain members of the same category. For instance, the "Nonhuman Victims—Socially Acceptable" cell contains only two kinds of killing—hunting and butchering. What are the differences between them? A brainstormed list of contrasts might help:

HUNTING	BUTCHERING
seasons	no seasons
many arbitrary rules of conduct based upon a notion of sportsmanship	rules of conduct based upon a concern for sanitation and humaneness but not really on sportsmanship
victims are wild animals	victims are usually domesticated animals
final motive is sport	final motive is survival—and profit
certain legally prescribed weapons	weapons are not prescribed; indeed, "weapons" seems to be a strange term here; "tools" sounds more fitting

HUNTING	BUTCHERING
a prescribed limit—usually one mammal per hunter per season and so many birds per hunter per day	no prescribed limit—supply and demand controls the rate of kill

The process of contrast could continue far beyond this, but perhaps by now a pattern has already begun to emerge: Unlike butchering, hunting seems to be governed by rules that are based not so much upon practical concerns as upon arbitrary, more or less aesthetic, almost "magical" concerns. Hunting has an attribute that might be called "ritualistic," whereas butchering has not—and this quality appears to subsume most of the specific contrasts listed above. Thus "ritualistic" versus "nonritualistic" might be useful categories. (This is just one of many possibilities such as "done for pleasure" versus "not done for pleasure"; "paid to do" versus "not paid to do.") The matrix produced by the Idea Machine could now be revised as Figure 5 illustrates.

KINDS OF KILLING

	Human Victims	Nonhuman Victims	
Socially Acceptable	justifiable homicide	butchering	Nonritualistic
	execution war	hunting	Ritualistic
Socially Unacceptable	accidental homicide euhanasia (?) abortion (?)	abortion (?)	Nonritualistic
	suicide[1] murder[2] religious sacrifice₁	bullfighting (in U.S.) religious sacrifice₂	Ritualistic

FIGURE 5. An eight-cell matrix that sorts kinds of killing on the basis of three attributes. The subscripts indicate different kinds of religious sacrifice. The question marks indicate some indecision about the victim in abortion and about the social acceptability of abortion and euthanasia.

[1] Suicides practically always contain a certain element of ritual: The suicidist often leaves a note; while waiting for the gas he often makes himself comfortable; on the rooftop there is often an elaborate pre-jump ritual, and so on.
[2] Murder is sometimes very ritualistic. Other times, as in more or less spontaneous crimes of passion, it appears to be nonritualistic. Notice how the question of premeditation enters in here.

One can add attributes until he is either worn out or until he has achieved the precision desired. But perhaps the foregoing is enough to demonstrate the two major uses of the Idea Machine. First, it provides a systematic way of looking at a certain subject matter and encourages an increasingly precise use of terms. Second, it encourages questions that can lead to new insights, new ideas, new things to say.

USING THE IDEA MACHINE

Pick a key term from your source material or from your own draft and apply the Idea Machine to it. If you can't think of anything else to write, explain what you are doing—and why. Try the following procedure:

1. Brainstorm a list of terms similar and more or less parallel to your target term.

2. Sort out the list, looking for shared attributes, marked differences, and items that do not actually seem to fit your list. Don't forget the help that the list of interrogatives mentioned on page 61 can provide. And do not be afraid to start out noticing and saying the simplest and most obvious things. The more complex ideas and insights can come later.

3. Set down what in your opinion appear to be the two most crucial attributes that run through the items in your list. With the use of these two attributes construct a four-cell matrix.

4. Place the items from your list into the cells of the matrix. If you have any blank cells, try to fill them in. Try to get three or four items inside each cell. The focused probing that you will have to do to come up with several examples for each cell can be a productive source of insight and draft.

5. Fix on one cell and find a third attribute that distinguishes among the items in that cell. Construct an eight-cell matrix.

6. Try different combinations. Remember that you can start all over with an entire new set of attributes at any time and can come up with an entirely different analysis and classification.

7. Write notes to yourself as you work the machine. Questions,

new distinctions, hunches, seeming contradictions, flashes of insight—all are valuable zero draft.

NOTES

1. Immanuel Kant, "Introduction," *Critique of Pure Reason,* trans. Norman Kemp Smith (New York: St. Martin's Press, 1965), p. 47.
2. The discussion of componential analysis in this chapter by necessity simplifies complications and blurs distinctions in order to set down a useful method of investigation. The following articles develop the matter more fully:
  Ward H. Goodenough, "Componential Analysis," *Science,* 156 (June 1967), 1203–1209.
  Kenneth L. Pike, "A Linguistic Contribution to Composition," *College Composition and Communication,* 15 (May 1964), 82–88.
  Hubert M. English, Jr., "Linguistic Theory as an Aid to Invention," *College Composition and Communication,* 15 (October 1964), 136–140.
3. René Descartes, *Rules for the Direction of the Mind,* trans. E. S. Haldane and G. R. T. Ross, vol. 31, *Great Books of the Western World,* ed. Robert M. Hutchins (Chicago, London, Toronto: Encyclopaedia Britannica, 1952), p. 14.

6 THE DIALOGUE

Since the days of Plato, philosophers have found the dialogue to be a natural and congenial form for their writing. Though it is used less frequently in fields such as economics and chemistry, it can work well any time there are solid differences of opinion. Since the form has been used for centuries to show the conflict of ideas, some instructors in some classes—especially philosophy professors—may be willing to let the final form of your paper remain as dialogue. For other teachers you may have to change the dialogue into monologue, a task that sounds more difficult than it is (see pages 74–75).

Even when writing for professors who insist on the monologue form, the dialogue can be valuable during the drafting phase. Very often students, even ones with severe inhibitions when drafting essays, find that the dialogue form releases a flow of words so large that twenty pages can be written at a single sitting. Once they get started, most students seem to enjoy writing in the dialogue form. Some appear to like it simply because it uses up paper faster than do other forms. Some like to write dialogue because they can draft in short spurts, since the form lends itself to being dropped and picked up again, like a floating bull session, whose perennial topic can be dropped and returned to the next day, the next week, and next month.

Some students appear to like dialogue because certain taboos of the standard essay form can be violated freely. There is no problem with sentence fragments, for fragments occur in conversation naturally. There is no concern with transitions, for it is typical of conversation that a voice pops in with a new idea at almost any time. There are no problems with paragraphing, for paragraphs don't exist in dialogue. Unfortunately, it is also true that some few students don't manage dialogue well at all. But, still, most of the time drafting in dialogue does have a relaxing, loosening effect that encourages a copious flow of words.

When one writes in dialogue he relies upon his innate ability to mimic, an ability delighted in by children, but one that is apt to be neglected as a person grows older. In his teens one is apt to settle upon a limited self-image and to restrict his expressiveness to a few habitual roles, developed more to protect his self-image from bruises than to help him become a fully articulate and fluent adult. The dialogue form gives students a chance to try on some new voices; for example, it can be an opportunity to mimic, perhaps with certain delicious malice, the academic voices that now surround them. A student who may have fallen into a pose of limited articulateness and whose writing voice may not have changed since ninth grade might find that, if he puts his mind to it, he can write sentences that sound just like those his political science professor might have spoken.

Because of its reliance upon the innate ability to mimic, drafting in dialogue offers a gentle way to disengage self-expression from the restraints of outmoded and restrictive self-images. For instance, a student might write lines for himself in his dialogue that match the somewhat fumbling and inarticulate self-image he has been carefully preserving. But in the same dialogue he might also write lines for an older friend who is more sophisticated and fluent. He might learn from this that he, himself, is more like his friend than he had realized.

CHOOSING THE VOICES

When you start a dialogue, you need a cast of two or three characters. It is probably better not to get involved with more than three.

What characters should be used? Because you must mimic, you ought to use people you know and have heard (or read). You, yourself, can be one of the voices. For the second person, choose someone who represents the kind of reader you have in mind. Writing is done, for the most part, because somebody needs to know something, whether he admits it or not. Your reader, then, can be envisioned as somebody who needs to know what you have to say. To get the dramatic potential that is implicit in dialogue to work for you, choose as a reader someone who is slightly hostile to your opinions on the subject. He need not be an opponent, just someone who differs with you enough to make you work for his agreement. He should be someone whose opinion you respect enough to want to show him how you think —even though he sees things differently. A slightly hostile reader can push you to levels of achievement that you might not attain in an easier rhetorical situation. It is a little bit like the situation of the mile-runner who finds that he can run his best race only when his competition pushes him.

For the third voice—if you choose to have three—consider using someone who represents the subject and who knows more about it than either you or your reader, such as an author or a professor whose voice you know from lectures or discussions. If you use an author, say Eldridge Cleaver on black militancy, try to use actual lines from his works, just to stay honest. Imitate only when you cannot find an appropriate statement in the author's books. If you use a professor, have whatever fun you want with him, but try not to caricature his position too much.

To sum up: The recommended cast of characters for a dialogue consists of (1) you, (2) your reader, and (3) a voice that represents your subject. Of course, that third voice is apt to dominate the conversation. But that doesn't matter as long as the other voices ask active, responsive questions and are also asked questions by the expert. The trick is to make each voice listen to the others, so that answers are aimed directly at the question and the questioner. As final author of the voices, of course, you should listen to the entire cast: your own voice, your reader's, and your subject's.

All sorts of variations can be worked out on this basic pattern. You might decide to leave yourself out of it. One student did just that when she wanted to write what she thought her minister would say on a particular ethical problem. (She thought his approach to a number of problems was dead wrong.) In her dialogue she pulled out of the scene and left the minister to face the voice of Jesus Christ alone. Rather than trying to put words into the mouth of Christ, she simply used quotations from the New Testament. Naturally, the passages she used from Christ's statements were on her side. The minister lost.

CHOOSING A SETTING

Once you have decided upon the voices for a dialogue, put them into some kind of setting, some sort of natural situation, and get them talking to one another. Dormitory rooms, coffee shops, local taverns, long-distance buses, the banks of rivers—all these and more have been used by students as settings for their dialogues. A setting includes both the physical surroundings in which the conversation takes place and the social situation—that is, the reasons these people are in this place at this particular time. You should consider not only where the people are, but why they are there. Is it simply a coffee break between classes? Did one of the people deliberately seek out the other? A definite, motivated setting for the dialogue helps keep the conversation natural. The situation can be used to ease you into the dialogue, and the circumstances of the setting can suggest how to end the conversation naturally: a class is about to start, the bus gets to the station, and so forth.

If you have a physical setting and the social situation well imagined, there is no need to describe the setting or the situation separately. The dialogue itself will tell the reader as much as he needs to know about what is going on and where it is. Try to visualize the scene as vividly as you can as you write the dialogue, but begin writing the dialogue, not the descriptions.

DIALOGUE STYLE

The natural basis for all dialogues is normal conversation—over coffee cups, in dormitories, in conference rooms, at breakfast tables. Sometimes dialogue is drafted by a writer who is working by himself, imaginatively projecting himself into the various voices. Sometimes it is useful to work with friends on such a project, to sit down and talk with someone who is as much as possible like one of the voices in the dialogue. You might tape-record the conversation and draft from the tape, or you might simply rely on your memory. In any case, the dialogue that is written down can grow out of an actual dialogue.

But don't strive too hard for the "naturalness" of normal conversation. The "natural" voices of a conversation put in a dialogue are apt to be oddly disappointing when read in cold print. The harder a writer tries to mimic "real" conversation, the more inane it can seem, whereas the harder he aims at exposition, the more artificial it can sound.

Tape-recorded interviews or panel discussions, such as those in *Playboy* and *Redbook,* are heavily edited. Not even the dramatist writing for the stage writes completely "real" conversation. To do so would be to risk boredom and inanity. The "natural" sound in writing is a deliberate, though not always conscious, artifice. To create language that reads naturally, you can't trust your ears alone. Even dialogue form, when written to be read, is prose—and prose is not structured like the oral language of everyday speech. Any given sentence in a dialogue or a play should be a sentence that could actually have been spoken; what is implausible is that so many things are said so well, so much to the point, in so short a time. Written dialogue compresses into real time sentences that—because they were written and not spoken—were absolved from the pressures of real time. A writer can take three hours or more to write a line that is read in three seconds. The written dialogue idealizes an intellectual event—and, therein lies the power of a good dialogue.

STARTING THE DIALOGUE

The clash of minds in a dialogue can force hidden ideas and feelings about a subject to the surface. In the example that follows, the surfacing of such ideas led the writer to discover that his original stance toward his subject was less firm than he thought. The student, writing a paper critical of hippies, said at one point in his zero draft, "Hippies are just interested in calling attention to themselves." Like an iceberg, such a sentence—indeed, *any* sentence—reveals only a fraction of itself to immediate gaze. Much of its mass lies hidden, in the form of unstated but inevitable assumptions and implications.

Testing Assumptions and Implications

The dialogue form is a natural way to force implications and assumptions to the surface. A brainstorming session can begin to get out into the open some of the mass underlying the statement about hippies:

1. This statement assumes that one can speak intelligently of someone else's motives.
2. It assumes that hippies are all motivated by more or less the same thing.
3. The word "just" implies that there is something wrong with people who are attempting to call attention to themselves.
4. The statement implies that hippies are either liars or else do not understand their own motives, for they don't talk about themselves in such language.

Notice that a voice hostile to this intended point of view could pick up any one of these statements and use it to probe and attack that point of view. But let us concentrate on the third statement to demonstrate the kinds of things that can happen once the voices in a dialogue argue about an assumption or implication. In the following dialogue Duke speaks for the writer's point of view. Peone, a hippy, is the reader and, not too surprisingly, is somewhat hostile. Notice that in the dialogue the writer really tries to give Peone a chance, even tries to empathize with him.

PEONE: What's wrong with people trying to call attention to themselves?

DUKE: I didn't say there was anything wrong with it.

PEONE: Yeh, man, you did too. You said *just*. You said *just* trying to call attention to themselves. And that means that there's something wrong with trying to get a little attention.

DUKE: Well, okay, there is something wrong with it. It's like telling off-color jokes or like a little kid throwing a tantrum, *just* to get attention. It's a pretty stupid way for an adult to act.

PEONE: Hold it, man. Why do you think those girls at the table over there are wearing their skirts so short? And why are they wearing perfume? Why do you think ol' Jocko over there in his letterman's sweater turns out for the team? They all want attention. You want to put them down?

DUKE: No, that's different.

PEONE: How?

DUKE: Well, it is. Everybody knows that it is. That's all.

PEONE: The fact is, ol' buddy, that you like the way those girls attract attention. And you like ol' Jocko's technique, too. That's all. You like their way, but you don't like mine. What's the difference? You like the girls because they're decorative? I'm decorative. You like Jocko because he gives you something to get excited about? I give you something to get excited about.

By now the dialogue is well under way. Peone has made it clear that Duke cannot condemn something as a demeaning, juvenile thing just because it attracts attention to the doer. Thus, in a sense, Peone asks the question, What is the difference between acceptable and unacceptable devices? The kind of thought that goes into the answer to that question can prove to be fruitful because by now it has become clear that Duke does not dislike hippies just because they are striving for recognition (if they are). Rather, what he dislikes is the particular *way* they are striving for recognition. Seeing that simple distinction is a step in the right direction.

Exploring the Range of Variation

There is another kind of questioning that can keep the words flowing. The technique is based upon determining the range of variation for a given term. That is, you ask, "In what way and to what degree can *X* be changed before it is no longer *X?*" This type of questioning offers a way of pinning down the crucial attributes that go to make up the category labeled by the word in question. And this kind of questioning provides another way of probing your subject to produce new ideas and more draft—as long as you keep writing down your questions and answers. The technique can be illustrated by the following, perhaps somewhat trivial, example: The terms "shirt" and "sweater" are used with ease and precision. But what, precisely, is the difference between a shirt and a sweater? How much can a shirt be varied before it becomes a sweater? A sweater is made out of heavier material, but does that mean that if a shirt is made out of heavy material it is actually a sweater? Apparently not, because some so-called shirts are just as heavy as, if not heavier than, some so-called sweaters. Sweaters are usually worn over shirts, but does that mean that if a sweater is worn without a shirt under it, it is no longer a sweater? If a so-called sweater is worn under a so-called shirt, has the sweater been changed into a shirt, and vice versa?

Sometimes the difference between the two things can be pinned down—that is, the limits of variation and the identity of crucial attributes can be established. But more often a sweater is a sweater and a shirt is a shirt and everybody knows it but nobody really knows exactly why. What is the difference between a chair and a stool? a bush and a tree? a fruit and a vegetable?

So far we have been talking about concrete things, but the technique works equally well, if not better, when dealing with more abstract concepts. For instance, at what point does heroic self-sacrifice become a suicidal death wish? What kinds of things can a political moderate do before he would be called a liberal, or a conservative, or a radical? At what point does education become propaganda? At what point does liberty become license? moderation become obstructionism? a childlike joy become childish irresponsibility?

In their dialogue so far, Peone and Duke have come to a distinction that lends itself to an examination of the range of variation: At what point does an acceptable form of attention-getting become unacceptable? Their dialogue might continue from where it left off.

DUKE: Well, some things are okay as ways to get attention and some things aren't.
PEONE: So what's the big difference?
DUKE: For one thing, certain ways are accepted and established—like trying to look attractive or playing football.
PEONE: You mean to say that any way is okay so long as it is "accepted and established"? And besides, aren't you going to leave any room for some new ways? We all have to go along doing things the accepted and established ways. We'd still be British colonials if guys like you had their way.
DUKE: No, wait a minute. There have to be new ways, sure, but even the new ways have to fall inside certain limits. They can't be too offensive. Like, for instance, not taking baths.

PEONE: I see. For me not to take a bath with super-duper antiseptic soap is to be offensive. For you to whip around in a gas-guzzling car that's six times as powerful as it has to be, making noise, endangering my life and limb, and dumping exhaust crud into the air—that's okay. Your big-man, sex-symbol cigarettes can make my eyes water and make the air stink—that's okay, too.

DUKE: Now wait a minute. There is a difference here. Some things are okay and some things aren't. Okay things are accepted by most people, not okay things aren't.

PEONE: That's what old de Tocqueville called "tyranny of the majority."

On and on the discussion could go. Again, there might be no final answer in the search for the crucial distinction. It is seldom possible to draw the line and say, "On the left is X, and on the right is Y." But the whole point, not too surprisingly, is precisely that the final answer is not so important as the intellectual quest for the answer.

FROM DIALOGUE TO MONOLOGUE

If your final paper must be in a standard monologue form, the shift from dialogue to monologue is usually easy to make. After listening carefully to the voices of your dialogue, choose the one that seems most appropriate for the assignment and let that voice do all the talking. Because it has been listening to the other voices, that voice can now anticipate their questions and objections in monologue form. Not only that, but the voice you choose might find that it has learned something from the others and that its original stance is no longer what it used to be—as the writer of the dialogue on hippies found out when it came time to cast it into its final monologue form:

> Hippies are often criticized for acting like small children, throwing a kind of temper tantrum simply to attract attention. The charge may be true. But we all try in our own ways to attract attention. We dress and ornament ourselves, we play football, we drive the sportiest car we can afford—all ways of attracting attention.

What we have to recognize is that there are certain ways of attracting attention that are acceptable and even valuable, and there are certain ways that are not. It may be hard to explain exactly where to draw the line, but it is not hard to tell when somebody has gone far beyond it. The young man who walked into a beauty parlor and killed three customers, just to attract attention, was obviously far beyond the line. I think that certain things the hippies do are far beyond the line, too—the hard drugs, for instance, but most important, the arrogant rejection of *everything* represented by the "square" world. . . .

A NOTE ON LOGIC

It was out of the clash of dialogue in Athens more than two thousand years ago that formal logic received public form. Formal logic is the intellectual tool especially designed to check the implications of statements. In its full form it encompasses so much that it can distract a novice writer beyond recovery. There is, however, a small text that introduces a student writer to just enough of just the right material from logic to be of help. It is Ray Kytle's *Clear Thinking for Composition* (New York: Random House, 1969).

7 HOW TO USE EXAMPLES AND ANALOGIES

When students are admonished to use more examples, it is very often because their generalizations lack the support of specific and concrete detail. Generalizations, to be persuasive, need evidence, and examples can be used to provide that evidence. For instance, in the second and third sentences below are examples that support the generalization in the first:

> Textbooks are getting too expensive—and too heavy. This quarter my psychology text cost me eight dollars and weighs two pounds. My English text cost ten dollars and weighs almost three pounds!

When a scientist deals with such examples, they are called "specimens." The biologist, for example, presents a frog preserved in a bottle; the botanist, a pressed flower; the geologist, a piece from an interesting rock formation. But frogs, flowers, and rocks are hard to present directly in term papers.

While most often a writer must rely on words to describe a specimen offered as evidence, there are, however, media other than words that can be employed for providing concrete and specific examples. Photographs and drawings are stand-bys and are still very useful. Tape recordings also can be helpful for the presentation of certain kinds of specimens—in speech classes, for instance, or in literature classes, where a student can turn in a written analysis of a poem as well as an oral interpretation of it in which he tries to dramatize his analysis. Tape-recorded examples can be valuable, too, for the student of the social or behavioral sciences who is dealing with interviews in which it is important for the audience to catch the interviewee's intonations.

A student once wrote a term paper on the various textures used in making pottery. She made a small pot and turned it in with the paper. The first sentence of the paper said, "Pick up the pot and feel the bottom." The entire paper was simply an exploration of that single pot in which she had demonstrated a number of different textures. It was a good paper, and a good pot—still being used by the instructor as a pencil holder. The point is that examples come in an infinity of shapes and forms. Don't be afraid to use your imagination in your quest for ways of presenting them.

ON ANALOGIES

Most of the time the admonition "Use examples" means little more than "Be specific" or "Be concrete"—that is, add details that will support a generalization. But very often exemplification leads to more than specific or concrete language. Sometimes the example carries with it a sense of "analogy." Analogy is a special kind of comparison, a recognition of similarity between two items or events. In the more striking analogies the two things compared are on the surface markedly dissimilar, and the analogy highlights a surprising similarity within apparent differences. An analogy compares two seemingly dissimilar things so as to highlight those attributes shared by them. It says that X is the same as Y in such-and-such respects, and it implies that, since the two things are alike in certain known respects, they are probably alike in certain as yet unknown respects as well.

One common use of analogy is the *model,* which explains one thing in terms of something more tangible. This kind of model is used widely in the sciences to explain something, rather than to describe it. The model that presents the atom as the same as a miniature solar system is a case in point. The atom, obviously, does not look like a miniature solar system, but if we think of it that way, some things about it can be better explained.

Another common use of analogy is in *poetic metaphor*—such as in Shakespeare's analogy "All the world's a stage . . ." from *As You Like It* (II, vii). In this analogy Shakespeare is not trying to describe the appearance of life, but rather to explain something about its quality. The world does not look like a stage any more than an atom looks like a solar system; it is just that sometimes real life feels like the artificial life on a stage, as Shakespeare goes on to detail when he expands his metaphor.

Analogies explain things through images by pointing out unexpected similarities and unities. In the introduction to his *A Comprehensive World: On Modern Science and Its Origins,* Jeremy Bernstein describes the explanatory power of analogy:

> The great physicists have all been masters of what has come to be known as *"Gedanken* experiments"—experiments existing only in the mind, unperformed and probably unperformable, which, when contemplated, put physical ideas into new and striking juxtapositions. For example, Newton became aware of the universal character of the law of gravitation by imagining an apple tree so big that its branches held the moon like an apple. Just as an apple in a small tree falls to the earth, so, to Newton, must the moon be falling in the gravitational field of the earth. . . .[1]

Sigmund Freud maintained that his theory of sublimation grew out of an analogy suggested by a cartoon he saw in a German magazine. The first picture in the cartoon showed a young girl herding a flock of geese with a stick; the second picture, composed like the first, showed the same girl, now grown into a woman, herding a flock of young girls with a parasol.

Again and again, great creative insights in art and science have stemmed from images coupled with analogies. Two dissimilar things, one usually an image, have been seen as somehow the same as one another to the extent that the image—that is, the more concrete item —could be used to explain and to exemplify the other. As Jacob Bronowski says:

> A man becomes creative, whether he is an artist or a scientist, when he finds a new unity in the variety of nature. He does so

by finding a likeness between things which were not thought alike before, and this gives him a sense both of richness and of understanding. The creative mind is a mind that looks for unexpected likenesses.[2]

CREATING AN ANALOGY

Even though analogy is central to creativity, there is no reason to feel that it is so exalted a thing that you must be incapable of it. Striking an effective analogy depends as much on being willing to try as on anything else. Try, even at the risk of producing some clinkers. One very simple technique that at times can produce striking analogies is very easy, almost gamelike. It has been dubbed "Winging It" to suggest its improvisational character.

"Winging It"

To "wing it" is to compare your subject with the first concrete thing that pops into your head, the wilder the better. For instance, if your subject is beauty, write down the paradigm "Beauty is like _____ because _____." Then put some concrete noun into the first blank. In the simplest form of "winging it" the concrete nouns can be chosen at random. You might simply try objects that you can see as you sit in your room. For instance, "Beauty is like a ballpoint pen." The problem now is to fill in the second blank by forcing yourself to see some point of similarity between beauty and the ballpoint pen. Perhaps you come up with "Beauty is like a ballpoint pen because you never know when it is going to run out on you." Or perhaps "Beauty is like a ballpoint pen because you usually lose it before you use it all up." As odd as it might seem at first, you can almost always discover striking similarities between even the most disparate things. Why is violence like an electric lamp? love like a rug? sin like a piece of chalk? a college curriculum like a double-decker bunk?

In this simplest form "winging it" only accidentally leads to an analogy, but it always can produce valuable zero draft—if you keep writing. It can force your mind to discern similarities that can lead to a greater understanding of your subject. If you are lucky, you might produce a comparison good enough to use in your final draft—perhaps even one that can form the linking image for an entire passage—or even an entire paper. If you are truly lucky, you might hit upon something that goes beyond the descriptive power of simple comparison and takes on the explanatory power of analogy. However, you can increase the likelihood of creating an analogy if you control the choice of concrete nouns. Pick those nouns that seem to have some fairly obvious association with your more abstract subject. Don't be afraid of starting with the obvious association, but try to look behind and beyond the initially obvious by looking for more subtle points of similarity. How is being addicted to drugs like being a slave—other than in the obvious loss of freedom? How *is* love like a warm puppy? How is war like an ashtray—other than in the presence of ashes?

And finally, even if you should draw a blank, "winging it" can be rather fun, especially in small-group brainstorming sessions. And it is good exercise as well—rather like intellectual isometrics.

Sprouting Analogies

It is possible to learn to recognize in draft that is already written analogies that are just beginning to sprout. Watch your draft for comparative words such as "like" and "as" and for phrases such as "_____er than" or "so _____ that"—for such words and phrases often mark sprouting analogies. Sometimes the analogies are not so obvious. In such cases it is helpful to pinpoint certain key concepts in the draft and then to list the most important things said about them. Very often the list of attributes of a subject will suggest the kind of image an analogy can be built upon. This technique is nicely illustrated in the following passages of zero draft, in which a student sets in opposition two very general and abstract concepts, science and mysticism:

> When the mystics contrast "reality" with "appearances," I feel the word *reality* has more of an emotional than a logical significance. To the mystic reality means what is important. When he says that time is "unreal," he means that sometimes it is important to conceive the universe as a whole, as the Creator. At such times all process falls within a completed whole. Past, present, and future all exist, and at the same time. The present does not have that preeminent reality which it has to our normal ways of

apprehending the world. If mysticism is to be interpreted this way it represents an emotion and not a fact. It doesn't really assert anything so it can neither be confirmed nor rejected by science. When mystics do make positive assertions, I feel it is because of their inability to separate emotional importance from scientific validity. This view of mysticism is not unacceptable to the scientific intelligence, for there is an element of wisdom to be learned from the mystical way of feeling that doesn't seem to be attainable in any other way. Even the cautious investigation of truth by science has been fostered by the spirit of reverence which is so characteristic of mysticism.

The two key topics are clearly mysticism and science, but the language of this passage is so general and abstract that it evokes no single, strong image upon which to base an analogy. What is needed is some way to shift from the abstract and general to the more concrete. One helpful way of making such a shift is to use *personification*—that is, to speak of abstract generalities as if they were human beings. The problem is to find a personification of science and mysticism that is capable of generating some analogical force. In such a case, the first thing to do is to list some of the things attributed to the major topics:

MYSTICISM	SCIENCE
Emotional significance	Logical significance
Emotion	Fact
Emotional importance	Scientific validity
Way of feeling	Scientific intelligence
Spirit of reverence	Cautious investigation of truth

Notice that attributes of mysticism include such things as emotion, feeling, and mystery—all rather feminine characteristics. Science, on the other hand, has logic and factuality and reason attributed to it—things most often thought of as more typically masculine. Perhaps, then, a man-woman personification would be helpful—with mysticism as the emotional, feeling, mysterious woman, and science as the factual, logical, rational man. There is even some detail in the passage that would suggest the nature of the relationship between the man and the woman: There is basically a disagreement, although mysticism neither reveals nor asserts anything, but just trusts her own feelings. This personified disagreement begins to sound rather like the classical encounter between the businesslike, masculine mind and the quiet, mysterious, feminine intuition.

EXPANDING AN ANALOGY

Given this basic personification, the next step is to elaborate or expand upon the analogy by asserting and exploring as yet unrecognized points of similarity and difference between woman and mysticism on one hand, man and science on the other. Set up the analogy in the form *"X is like Y":* "The relationship between mysticism and science is like the relationship between a man and a woman." Then ask such questions as the following:

1. How are *X* and *Y* obviously similar?
2. How are they obviously different?
3. What do these points of similarity and difference suggest about *X?*
4. Picking an attribute of *Y* not noted so far, ask yourself in what sense *X* can be said to share it. If *X* is said to share it, what lines of thought are opened up?

This kind of elaboration is useful in a number of ways. First, it makes it possible to test the "fit" of the basic analogy and thus the cogency of the personification. It also makes explicit some of the implications of the analogy—implications that may or may not then be presented explicitly to the reader. And finally, it helps the writer fix his conscious mind on the subject and produce more draft.

Once an analogy is set up, elaborating it is remarkably easy. The two things linked through the analogy obviously must share at least one attribute—or be similar in at least one way—but they cannot share all attributes, for if they did so, they would be the same thing. As you elaborate an analogy, look for both the similarities and the differences, both those attributes shared and those not shared. In this way you are forced to take a closer look at attributes that might otherwise be ignored.

The technique is simply to fix upon one attribute of the topic of the personification and to see in what sense it can be said to be shared by the original topic—in this case, mysticism. For instance, woman is often thought of as the source of life; is there any sense in which the same statement can be made of mysticism? Woman is often thought of as the weaker sex, and yet evidence suggests that in certain ways she is much stronger than man. Are there any ways in which it can be claimed that, although on the surface mysticism is "weaker" than science, actually she is "stronger"? Statistically, women live longer than men. Can the same be said of mysticism as compared with science? This question raises certain specific subquestions for some reading and study: For instance, historically, which is older, mysticism or science? Traditionally, men are taken to be more concerned with power—guns, big cars, powerful machines, big factories, big business, and so forth. Women, on the other hand, are usually thought of as more concerned with everyday things—food, the home, the family. How can these differences be extended into the mysticism-science contrast? Traditionally, woman, as the mother, is thought of as being more concerned about the child than is the man, or father. In what sense could it be suggested that mysticism is more concerned than is science about her "children"?

The process of elaborating the analogy that lies behind the personification could go on and on. It is quite simple—merely a matter of checking off points of similarity and difference. Many of the lines of elaboration might not be edifying—might serve only to remind us of the limits of analogical reasoning. But some of them could produce helpful insights. Some of the specifics, the images, might even show up in the final draft. The imagery of the personification could be very useful for fixing the tone of the discussion. Indeed, the man-woman personification might prove to be a master analogy, one that could be used to link the various sections of an entire paper. Such a master analogy could introduce the discussion, tie it together throughout the main exposition, and finally bring it together at the end.

But even if the analogy should not prove to be so permanent, it at least forces a close look at the main topics and leads to questions that in turn lead to things that should be explained to the reader. Thus the imagery suggested in the perscnification can help the writer explain his subject.

The following bit of zero draft—dealing with birth control and the population explosion—illustrates a somewhat similar opportunity to use analogy:

> Our chances of survival are being threatened. Threatened because mankind dares not use the one gift he possesses among all others. This gift is his intelligence and he will choose to ignore the use of it until life discontinues to cater to him. Space is running out. There are no new continents to open up. And the time is here for mankind to use this gift. Knowledge is not wisdom, we say. Yet in my opinion, the use of knowledge possessed is our only means of survival. Human happiness is our aim. Human foresight our necessity. It is the responsibility of all humanity to create those conditions ensuring happiness. Here I include an adequate diet, comfortable housing, general good health, jobs that make us proud of our contributions, and sufficient recreation. These conditions can be created through the intelligent control of family size. Only when man realizes these things and accepts them as his responsibilities will contentment and satisfaction with life reign. No longer can we ignore the problem and leave everything to chance.

Like the previous passage of zero draft, this one, too, turns on an opposition between two things—in this case between accepting gifts and accepting responsibilities. But for our immediate purposes, what is even more interesting is the tone of the passage. Notice the words and phrases that suggest a kind of emergency atmosphere:

> Our *chances* of *survival* are being *threatened*
> Mankind *dares* not use
> Space is *running* out
> *No* new continents to open up
> *The time is here*
> Our *only means of survival*
> *No longer* can we ignore

Notice how the phrases that carry this tone can also suggest certain analogies. The procedure to be followed here is a somewhat modified version of "winging it," discussed earlier. What else resembles the situation of emergency described in the passages of zero draft? "Our chances of survival are being threatened"—like the chances of the citizens of a besieged city? like the chances of rats in a trap? "Space is running out"—the way sand runs out of an hour glass? "The time is here"—the sand has run out? "No longer can we . . .

leave everything to chance"—like a gambler? Maybe, for it is a bad gambler who leaves everything to chance, who always counts on gifts of fate, on being catered to by life. A good gambler tries to improve the odds by making use of his intelligence to create (or at least improve) those conditions that make more happiness more likely. This thought trend can go on and on. The gambler-image seems to offer the basis of a good analogy, one that escapes the triteness of "the sands of time" and "like rats in a trap." It can subsume many of the ideas scattered throughout the zero draft. And like any good analogy, it can provide a unified terminology that can clarify the subject and control the tones—"odds," "bookmaking," "penny ante," "roulette," "chemin de fer," "shill"—the culture of the gambler is rich with words and images to concretize and unify the ideas in the passage as the analogy is elaborated.

THE DICTIONARY: A SOURCE OF ANALOGY

If you have trouble finding a promising analogy, your dictionary can offer considerable help. Most often all that is needed is a nudge or hint to get your mind under way—and a good desk dictionary is filled with little nudges and hints.

Etymologies

When it is hard to find the beginnings of an analogy in draft material, it is often because the language is so insistently abstract and general that there is no promising image upon which to fix. But most words, no matter how abstract they might be today in their meanings, harbor a latent image—and often a latent analogy. By tracking some of the key words back through their histories, using the etymologies in a desk dictionary or in a special etymological dictionary, you can often find a useful image or analogy. (See pages 44–46 for a discussion of dictionaries.)

For instance, if you were writing a paper about business and economics, it would be useful to know that our word "risk" comes from a Greek word *rhiza* meaning "cliff," and that etymologically "risk" is associated with the notion of sailing a boat around a cliff. The image and the analogy are clear. Similarly, the word "toil" comes from an old Latin name for a machine that was used for crushing olives, and "labor" comes from a word that signified a weight so heavy that it caused a man carrying it to stagger. Even such small hints as these are often all that is needed to set off a full-grown, productive analogy.

Again, if you were writing a paper on religion, it would be useful to know that our word "Lord" comes from the Anglo-Saxon word *hlafweard,* meaning, literally, "the loaf-warden"—that is, the keeper of the bread. ("Lady," by the way, comes from *hlafdige,* the kneader, or digger, of the bread.) If you elaborate the analogy between God and a "keeper of the bread," it would be rather natural for other helpful items to come to mind—for instance, the Biblical stories of heavenly manna, of the feeding of the multitudes, and of the communion of the Last Supper. In short, the analogy suggested by the etymology of "Lord" could open up a rich flow of questions and thoughts.

Some words have changed so drastically from their earlier meanings that their etymologies suggest what might be called "negative analogies." And for our purposes a negative analogy is just as good as a positive one. If you were writing a paper on creativity, for instance, although the word "expression" originally meant "a pressing out," you could argue that the word's most common current meanings—as in the phrase "to express oneself"—are opposed directly to the etymological sense of the word. You could argue that self-expression is not at all like a pressing out—for instance, it is nothing at all like squeezing toothpaste out of a tube or cider out of an apple. For one thing, once a person expresses himself, his mind is fuller, at least in the sense that his ideas are more clearly formulated, more accessible, more orderly, and more useful. This is quite unlike the image of the toothpaste tube or the apple, both left empty and dry after their "ex-pression."

Definitions

The list of current definitions of a given word can also reveal analogies latent within it. If you study the relationships between definitions of a given word, you can sometimes get some sense of the analogical leaps the word went through as its meanings were expanded and extended. One of these leaps might make a handy basis for a new analogy. Consider, for instance, the list of meanings for the word "nose," from its original denotation of that facial appendage to its more recent denotation of the front part of the head of a golf club. (This kind of searching can be helped along somewhat by checking the front matter of the dictionary to determine the order in which definitions are listed. Some dictionaries—*Webster's Seventh New Collegiate,* for instance—list definitions in a historical order, from the oldest to the newest. Other dictionaries—*The Random House Dictionary,* for instance—list definitions in an order from the most common to the least common.)

One word of advice: Whenever you use a dictionary as a source, whether you are tracking down etymologies or definitions, don't brag about it in your final draft. Try to avoid that old saw, "According to *Webster's,* blah-blah." There is something curiously anesthetic for readers in that tag line. Just go ahead and quietly use the results of your study and meditation. If you should find yourself needing to document dictionary material, go to the *Oxford English Dictionary* or, for more recent matters, to the unabridged *Random House Dictionary* or *Webster's Third International,* and indicate the source in parentheses in your text—for instance, "(OED)," "(RHD)," or "(*Webster's Third*)."

EXEMPLA: HOW TO USE THEM

An example that combines analogy with a scene can be called an "exemplum." Two common kinds of exempla are the *fable* and the *parable,* the scenes of which resonate with meanings more general and compelling than the concrete specifics of which they are composed. Aesop's famous fable about the tortoise and the hare, for instance, reaches out far beyond a simple story of a foot race. So, too, Christ's parable of the good Samaritan. Modern literary parables such as Robert Frost's "The Road Not Taken" cast forth ever-widening circles of meaning. In a similar, though less solemn, vein, the scenes of a modern parable such as Charles Schulz's *Peanuts* or a modern fable such as Walt Kelly's *Pogo,* also present details that are much bigger than themselves. And finally, that type of modern exemplum called the "case history" in psychology, psychiatry, sociology, or anthropology often resonates in exactly the same way.

Even if you finally decide not to include exempla in your final draft, they can be very useful because at their base are analogies—often very powerful analogies. For one thing, an exemplum, well placed, can help clarify and organize a cluster of heretofore muddled ideas. Along with this added clarity can come increased control over tone, because an exemplum can provide terms that have a single basic scene as their source. Such unified terms can help stabilize the tones of a passage by crowding out other terms that might carry vague, confusing, or conflicting images. Becoming sensitive to and learning to control exempla and using their analogical power to dominate stretches of prose are ways to fight gobbledegook.

An exemplum's meanings can be left implicit, or they can be drawn out and commented upon so that they are made explicit. When to spell out the implications of an exemplum and when to let the reader work things out for himself are problems in tactics that have no easy answers. In great part it all depends on the audience for whom you are writing. The artful way, of course, is to let the thing stand alone—as a short story or dramatic poem or even a well-told joke does—thereby inviting the reader into the discourse as an active participant rather than as a passive observer, since the implications have been left unstated.

Usually, however, in the kind of writing most often required in college, you need to be explicit in drawing out the implications of an exemplum. And even if you should decide not to make things explicit for your reader, it is a good idea to work out the implications of exempla in the privacy of the zero draft. The controlled musing and probing that such drafting requires lead to better control over material—and may uncover new lines of thought, new flashes of insight.

The following is an exemplum of far-reaching implications, which the student-writer chooses not to make explicit. The excerpt is part of the introduction to a theme in which the student sets down some of his basic philosophic assumptions, using a psychiatric case history to pull the reader up short—and also to prepare for the abstract and general language that follows:

> Like a number of my friends I am wary of the big abstractions and approach them cautiously, circling around them, sniffing cynically. Perhaps that is why I prefer parables to catechisms. For example, my personal scripture would include the following parable from a textbook of psychiatry. The text labels this parable "Case 3."

> An unmarried white woman, twenty-six years of age, sought advice from her physician because of certain unusual experiences that she had been undergoing. She was an attractive girl who had no physical complaints, but surprised the physician whom she consulted by stating, in the course of her history, that in spite of her attractive physical qualities, she experienced great difficulty in meeting people, especially strangers. She stated frankly that her life was an isolated one, but that for her, social life was unnecessary, because she enjoyed special illumination from above. She stated that this enabled her to penetrate facts and truths not perceived by ordinary people, that she enjoyed daily conversation with God, audibly hearing His voice calling her by name and revealing secret things. She indicated that among the directions thus divinely received were injunctions to spend a great deal of her time and energy in prayer and mortification. Accordingly, she was accustomed to refrain from food and drink several times a week, and to keep long vigils at night, watching and praying.
>
> As she thus gradually unfolded the amazing details of her life, her case was judged to be that of a true mystical soul, and she was so informed. She was encouraged to moderate her severities, but to continue to pay heed to the divine guidance she was receiving. A few days later, the young woman committed suicide.[3]

Several fine big abstractions slipped into this essay through that parable, so I shouldn't feel uncomfortable about the ones I am about to use.

The following is a very short exemplum from Albert Jay Nock's essay "The Disadvantages of Being Educated." The implications are specific and made explicit:

> Not long ago I met a young acquaintance from the Middle West who has done well by himself in a business way and is fairly rich. He looked jaded and seedy, evidently from overwork, and as I was headed for Munich at the moment, I suggested he should take a holiday and go along. He replied, "Why, I couldn't sell anything in Munich—I'm a business man." For a moment or two I was rather taken aback by his attitude, but I presently recognized it as the characteristic attitude of trained proficiency, and I saw that as things are it was right. Training had kept his demands on life down to a strictly rudimentary order and never tended to muddle up their clear simplicity or shift their direction.

Education would have done both; he was lucky to have had none.[4]

The following exemplifies quickly and explicitly what H. L. Mencken took to be the un-Christian character of legal punishment. Notice that he gave the characters letters instead of names, which produces an effect rather global in its range of implication, like that of the traditional allegory:

> A keeps a store and has a bookkeeper, B. B steals $700, employs it in playing at dice or bingo, and is cleaned out. What is A to do? Let B go? If he does so he will be unable to sleep at night. The sense of injury, of injustice, of frustration will haunt him like pruritus. So he turns B over to the police, and they hustle B to prison. Thereafter A can sleep. More, he has pleasant dreams. He pictures B chained to the wall of a dungeon a hundred feet underground, devoured by rats and scorpions. It is so agreeable that it makes him forget his $700. He has got his *katharsis*.[5]

The following two exempla are from a student's paper, an autobiography for a psychology class. The first exemplum is made rather explicit; the second is left quite implicit.

> Adolescence prepared me for later self-sufficiency and independence from my family. This preparation period called for physical growth and further education. Physical growth and maturation became criteria by which as an adolescent I graded my success in becoming an adult. I could do things I had never done before.

> We used to lie along the pool deck, charring our bodies evenly. Sometimes the sweat of our leisure would trickle down our necks, cooling the dip of our backs. We liked to jump into the pool, perhaps hoping the chlorine would purify us. Instead it burned our eyes and made them look as if we had been crying all afternoon. We tanned our bodies and strengthened our crawl stroke. Soon the lifeguard tested and passed us. We were allowed to leave the shallow for the deep end. Sometimes I felt very alone because I couldn't see the bottom. Looking back, there were times I almost drowned. But I learned to tread.

I feel that I have passed through a series of stages. At each stage an identity has emerged, and there has been a relatedness between the identities of each stage. Still, these identities always have a tentative quality, for each was a phase in becoming:

> I moved past the mailbox maze of childhood in dust-filled Keds, carrying white envelopes filled with bills and sticky, smelling envelopes filled with secrets. I was the mail getter, not knowing of debts to be paid or mystic messages. Finding the sky, I would raise the envelopes—looking for pearls, perhaps. The others were thick and blocked the sun. Then I would tuck the letters just right, so return addresses hemmed my pocket ridge. Didn't matter if people didn't know the letters weren't mine.

As the preceding passages illustrate, exempla can be either remembered, borrowed, or invented—just like the images and scenes used in contemplation. The best sources of remembered exempla are contemplative introspection and those sudden flashes of memory that bring back past scenes sometimes with startling clarity. The sources of borrowed exempla are as varied as one's own social and intellectual lives. They can be drawn from stories real and not so real that may have been heard or read. They can be fact or fiction.

Always keep alert for serendipity and its fruits. Listen and watch in all of your classes and during your reading for striking scenes and stories, anecdotes and incidents, that might be grist for your drafting. Keep your ears open, too, during arguments over coffee and during fits of just plain gossip. The newspaper can be a continual source for the bits of action that exemplify abstractions and make points. If there is nothing promising in the news section, try *Peanuts* or *Andy Capp*. Start filing likely candidates for future work. A binder filled with newspaper and magazine clippings can often provide you with just the nudge you need.

Do not forget the more traditional sources, either. The fables of Aesop and La Fontaine can often be put to good use—sometimes more or less as they are in the original, sometimes reworked to fit your particular purposes. Literature is in general a rich source for exempla. It is surprising how often the characters and events of Chaucer's *Canterbury Tales* recur today. So, too, the characters and events of Shakespeare's plays and of the famous novels. Literary allusion can provide you with powerful and compelling exempla. On the other hand, never underestimate your ability to invent and compose completely modern exempla of your own.

TWO FINAL SUGGESTIONS

Let's assume that the very worst has happened: You have tried all of the techniques discussed in this chapter, and you still have not found a basis for an analogy or exemplum. In such a fruitless situation it is quite likely that you have gotten too tied up with your problem. There is a rather painless remedy: Go to a movie and forget the whole thing. Give the powers of serendipity a chance. But more important, give in to inspiration's favorite rhythm—earnest courting followed by rest. Give the unconscious a chance. Quite possibly as you are walking home, a bit tired perhaps, the details of your problem will suddenly come together to form a new configuration. Very often, too often to be coincidental, the flash of insight, the solution, comes during a period in which you turn away from a problem after extended concentration on it.

If, during the attempt to find and elaborate analogies and exempla, you are careful to work with your strongest material, you can afford to spend considerable time working at the kinds of things discussed in this chapter. You can afford the time it takes to scratch out several pages of tentative draft material. The half page, or even ten lines, salvaged can include some of your best material. Learn to go after the strong points, giving them the time and thought necessary. To do so generates more good draft than does patching up material of less potential or importance. The process of drafting and redrafting—just like the process of editing—is a process in which you keep selecting out your strongest and most important material and building on it.

NOTES

1. Jeremy Bernstein, *A Comprehensive World: On Modern Science and Its Origins* (New York: Random House, 1967), pp. 9–10.

2. J. Bronowski, "The Creative Process," *Scientific American,* 199 (September 1958), 63.
3. The student's source for the case history is John R. Cavanagh and James B. McGoldrick, *Fundamental Psychiatry,* 2d ed. (Milwaukee: Bruce, 1958), pp. 30–31.
4. Albert Jay Nock, "The Disadvantages of Being Educated," in *The Borzoi College Reader,* ed. Charles Muscatine and Marlene Griffith (New York: Knopf, 1966), pp. 50–51.
5. H. L. Mencken, "The Penalty of Death," in *The Borzoi College Reader,* p. 256.

writing: plans, drafts, and revisions

HOW TO GET FROM ZERO TO FIRST DRAFT

8

Questioning and paraphrasing sources, writing descriptions of scenes that make concrete some issue within a subject, examining the crucial attributes of the categories and terms of a subject, writing in dialogue, developing analogies and examples—any of these drafting techniques may produce stretches of draft long enough and unified enough to be considered first-draft material.

SORTING THE DRAFT

Search the draft for passages that seem to be sufficiently long and unified. Use a scissors, when necessary, to cut a passage out from its zero-draft surroundings. Use whatever filing system suits you, but once again the loose-leaf binder system is recommended. At this stage simply put those promising passages in the front of a binder and leave the rest of the material in the back. As material is moved from back to front, start to sort it out tentatively by topics, using a few loose-leaf indexes.

The important thing here is not to fiddle too much: Look carefully at each passage, make a decision, and move on. The decisions are not irreversible. Work carefully, but don't agonize. Try to develop a momentum. Don't be surprised if the swatches of unified prose often do not correspond with the paragraphing in the draft, for paragraph indentations do not always mark off territory as routinely and securely as we might like to think. Do not hesitate, if necessary, to cut out a single sentence that somehow falls in the midst of alien territory. On the other hand, a long stretch of prose that happens to run 1½ feet long should be kept intact and handled like any other oversize piece of material—the top stapled to a backing sheet and the bottom folded up.

Watch for "leaners," those passages that seem to be as much about one topic as another so that it is difficult to decide where to place them. Put the "leaners" in a special packet, for later they may help provide transition between topics. They may even contain the beginnings of an insight about the relationships existing among topics.

Usually, as you sort through a draft, the number of new topics decreases, no new packets are formed, and the old, established packets get fatter. You may begin to notice similarities and connections unnoticed before. You may find that certain topics begin to subsume more and more of the material. When this occurs it is a sure sign that you are beginning to see more clearly what, in fact, you have written and what remains to be done.

The end result of the sorting phase should be a front section tentatively organized according to major topics and a back section with the remaining zero draft. Though the back section may hold passages that finally may prove to be unusable, it may also hold some that include too many ideas in too short a space to permit ready classification. This latter kind of rich, but brief, perhaps confused, material can be of great worth later in the editing—so leave everything there, throw nothing away until the final copy is completed. You never can tell ahead of time when and how some of this zero draft may prove to be significant.

As the sorting continues, topics will recur. Rich zero draft repeats itself a number of times in a number of ways. Sometimes a passage that repeats an earlier point will be long enough to be put up front; sometimes it will be short but will phrase an idea more accurately than anything in the longer passages. Those short passages of repetition belong up front, too, packeted with their longer fellows.

There also may be some passages that are skimpy but important —too short to be considered first-draft material, but improvable with further drafting. These passages, too, should be put up front. Be especially alert for scattered repetitions of the same ideas in skimpy passages. Add each recurrence of the idea to its packet up front. By the end of the sorting phase, the packet may be big enough and unified enough to have arrived at the level of first draft by sheer accumulation; usually, though, more drafting will still be required.

Now you might take the time to draft some more on the skimpy sections, fleshing them out a bit, drawing upon the added experience and understanding you have gained in the editing done so far. Or you might choose to wait until you have recaptured the momentum of drafting again before you attempt to add to those sections. In either case, with the skimpy but important passages up front, remember that the skimpy passages can be expanded by adding source material of various kinds or by invoking one or more of the drafting devices explained in Chapters 4 through 7.

TENTATIVE ORGANIZATION

With the pieces of zero draft filed in the back of the binder and the first-draft material gathered together by topics, the time has come to check the tentative organization in the front of the binder. Some larger clusters may emerge immediately. Even a glance may tell you that certain topics tend to cluster into a larger group. Remember, though, that there is hardly ever any *one* way that a clustering of topics can or must occur. As a matter of fact, it is a good idea, once you have worked out a likely-looking grouping—and perhaps a tentative sequence—simply to set that grouping and sequence aside and start all over again, forcing yourself to try to see three or four—or even more—different groupings and sequences.

This forced, but controlled and focused, tinkering with organization can juxtapose ideas in a fresh way—a way that might lead to a sudden, sharp insight about the connections among the topics. Don't let the gamelike quality of the activity fool you. It *is* rather gamelike, and it is also extremely important.

THE FIRST DRAFT

If you have followed the rule of thumb to zero draft three times as many words as you will finally need, and if you now discover after careful reading that you have actually written as much first-draft material as zero draft, then you are very nearly ready to rewrite your material into a full-fledged first draft. But before you do, reread the remnants of zero draft. Now that you have worked as much as you have with the draft, it is likely that you will see connections and ways to use some of those remnants that you could not see before. See which of the skimpy sections need to be built up, and jot down some notes about how you intend to flesh them out.

When you do sit down to write out a fresh copy of a first draft, try as much as possible to transmute the separate sections into one long, single, continuous unit. But do not be *too* concerned with questions of sequence. Simply gather the material into whatever sequence seems workable. The final decisions about sequence and transitions are better dealt with later on, after you have gained more control over the material. Use this rewrite to try out any fresh ideas about the organization of the material. This, your true *first draft,* should have considerably more order to it than did the zero draft. But do not be overly concerned if there should be gaps and jagged places in it still. They, once again, can be taken care of later.

THE COMMONPLACES

Sometimes material will stubbornly resist falling into a workable sequence of any kind. One type of unruly material wants to come out all a single, sticky mess—like cooked spinach. Another breaks apart into tiny, unkempt pieces—like a bucket of fishhooks. There are some standard patterns that can help discipline unruly draft. Classical rhetoricians call these patterns "commonplaces." They are not favorite subjects that are often discussed, as suggested by today's usage, but rather they are common ways of organizing material. Some of the classical rhetoricians worked out very elaborate catalogs of the commonplaces. (Aristotle, for instance, describes twenty-eight in his *Rhe-*

toric.) But we will restrict our discussion to just four. Each is common in modern prose, and each has proved to be useful to student-writers.

The Bitch-and-Pitch. Because of their position in life, students, like soldiers, are chronic bitchers. Again and again a draft falls neatly into two major parts: the complaint and the cure, the bitch and the pitch. The bitch-and-pitch is a favorite pattern for magazine articles, very common in *Reader's Digest, Playboy,* and *Harper's.* Just about every issue has at least one bitch-and-pitch article, all of which are variations on the "How to Save the _____" theme: "How to Solve the _____, Now!" "How to Prevent the _____ from _____ing Our Children."

The Inner-Outer. Another commonplace, used extensively in modern prose, is the grouping of material into interior versus exterior. In law and ethics the pattern is expressed usually in terms of private versus public, or the individual versus society. In psychology it becomes nature versus nurture, or heredity versus environment. In sociology it is the self versus society. In political science it comes out as domestic versus foreign. Again and again the list of topics can be grouped into matters of the inner versus matters of the outer. This grouping in turn usually calls attention to the interaction between the two. For instance, it would be possible to group the reasons for America's policy toward Russia into "inner reasons" and "outer reasons." Our policy reflects certain inner conditions—for instance, the fears many Americans have of the Soviet Union. The policy also reflects certain outer conditions—certain specific things that Russia has done. Clearly, these inner and outer conditions interrelate: To a certain extent Russian actions reflect American feelings, and American feelings reflect Russian actions. Once the writer has a grasp of the distinction between inner and outer and a sense of the complex and delicate interactions between the two, the material of his zero draft should begin to fall into a workable sequence.

The Before-and-After. A third commonplace is similar to that device very often used in cosmetic or diet-aid advertisements, in which picture number one shows Mrs. Smith "before," and picture number two shows her "after." Before-and-after is also the basic pattern of narrative, whether it be history or fiction. If you string enough before's and after's together, you end up with a *narrative,* or story. On the other hand, if you examine the relationship between "before" and "after," looking to see if there is any kind of cause-and-effect connection, the before-and-after pattern leads into *causal analysis.* Usually, then, the before-and-after will produce a third group that might be called *relationship*—that is, the connection between the "before" and the "after," a connection that is often causal.

The Same-and-Different. In this final commonplace the topics are grouped so as to show how two or more events or items are the same or different. In *comparison* the items are discussed so as to heighten the points of similarity between them, whereas in *contrast* they are discussed so as to heighten the points of difference.

Once you have a pattern spotted—even one so simple as the bitch-and-pitch, the inner-outer, the before-and-after, or the same-and-different—and once you apply it to the job of sorting out the fishhooks or separating the spinach, the major sections very often start to emerge. All that is needed is a bit of mental priming, a little something to get started with.

ZERO ZERO DRAFT

It also is possible that when you look over your zero draft for first-draft material there will not be much of it. There may be only a few patches of sustained, unified material. You may have a very zero zero draft. Such a thing is not at all uncommon, and although it is a bit melancholy, it is not grounds for despair.

Let's assume that the worst has happened: You have tried to create order out of seemingly unruly, chaotic material and have momentarily failed. The best tactic in such a situation is once again to court the Muse and the power of your unconscious, especially its power to work while you're asleep. Plan ahead a day or two and set aside a three- or four-hour period for writing—preferably in the morning. The night before that appointment, sit down and read all of your zero draft carefully, two or three times. Then go to bed. The next day get up and *without consulting your zero draft or source material,* sit down and write out the entire thing as best you can, from memory. Give your mind one more chance to shape and link the material, one more chance to develop unified passages. If you find yourself veering off on a slant quite different from anything you have done so far, fine; that might be the very slant that will begin to discipline the unruly material. Just give your mind a chance to rework the stuff and impress your personal order on it.

9 EDITING THE FIRST DRAFT: TOPICS AND SUMMARIES

The goal of editing can be stated quickly: to make certain that the reader will get a sense of satisfactory, intended form. Drafting provides the raw material; good editing discovers the appropriate form latent in that material.

The secret of good prose lies in repetition. Whether the intent is to entertain or persuade, in extended prose certain things are said over and over again. A theme is stated, varied, commented upon, restated. The sense of form that one gets from good prose depends upon this recurrence, not simply because things are repeated, but because the repetition sets up expectations in the reader. The first job of editing is to discern what recurs and to notice what expectations such recurrences will set up.

THE SUMMARY SENTENCE

In the early editing phase you will want to work with large blocks of first-draft material. You may stop to gather some sentences together or notice a particularly fine sentence and mark it, but do not spend time fiddling with commas, spelling, or sketchy diction. Aim at seeing the whole of what you have done and are to do. Avoid getting bogged down in detailed editing. That will come later. At this point the only individual sentences you should lavish time and effort on are those that summarize and state the theme of an entire section, for they are the ones that can do the most for your paper. For one thing, such sentences are used by a writer as his "topic" or "thesis" sentences. A writer will most certainly have a topic to start with—and he will have something to say about it. But what he is not apt to have is a clear statement of exactly what it is he will say, simply because he hasn't said it yet. Very often it is not until the editing stage, not until after the zero draft has been worked into a first draft that a writer begins to notice the often unstated themes that undergird many of his passages. Good thesis sentences are seldom written ahead of time. They are not sentences you start out with, but sentences you arrive at. To get to them, you draft first, then condense entire sections. A major part of editing is getting such sentences written and placed.

A well-placed, well-formed summary sentence can cast a glow of excellence across even ramshackle prose. Very often when reading somebody else's writing, the material seems to be fragmented, to come in bits and pieces. Then a climactic summarizing sentence comes, and the pieces fall into place. That single sentence encompasses and pulls together the entire passage. Without that sentence, the prose would have remained fragmented and unclear. With it, the prose is clear and tight. For that summary sentence states clearly the theme that holds the prose together.

The sentence that summarizes an entire section of a paper constitutes a mobile replica of the section. Because each statement of theme is more abbreviated than the section it summarizes, it is more mobile. Single sentences can be moved around a lot more easily than entire sections. It is this mobility that makes them so useful during editing.

Once you have a good summary sentence that neatly wraps up what you have been trying to say, then you can go back and place it in its setting. It can be used as one of those useful "thesis sentences" that obviously and usefully summarizes the thrust of the entire paragraph. But the power of summary sentences need not be limited to a single paragraph; many of them summarize more than one paragraph. The indentations that mark paragraphs do not correlate in any rigid, fixed manner with those powerful sentences that summarize minor and major sections of a manuscript and thus state its minor and major themes. These statements of theme are too useful to be rigidly controlled and circumscribed.

Placed inside the section they summarize, these sentences help give a sharp focus to that section. Placed after the section, toward the end of the paper, they provide useful recapitulation. Placed at the beginning of the paper, they become those promises that prompt a reader to expect exactly what will shortly be delivered. Summary sentences are powerful aids to form; they are the strongest links for plotting that a writer can desire. A half-dozen plump summary sentences, carefully placed, can carry an entire short theme. A dozen can carry an entire term paper.

Some of the summary sentences needed may already be lying in the first draft waiting to be spotted and placed where they belong. But most of them probably will have yet to be formed.

SECTIONING THE DRAFT

At this point, the editorial work facing the writer is twofold: one, he must determine just what are the minor and major sections of his paper so that, two, he can condense those sections into tightly packed summary sentences that explicitly state their themes. Following is a description of a procedure for getting those two jobs done. There is nothing original in the procedure; editors have been handling draft material in this way ever since paper became cheap enough to use so cavalierly. At first, the procedure will probably seem too elaborate, until you remember that it is a way to maintain the proper editorial distance from your material. It helps keep you honest with your own draft.

The following is a flexible sorting and labeling procedure that can be adjusted to fit the size of the job. It is a procedure of marking off and summarizing that works equally well with 2,000 or 200,000 words of draft. With really big jobs, you simply repeat the procedure, breaking the large mass of material into smaller and smaller, more manageable units.

Major Sections

First, try to get a sense of the total sweep of your draft by giving it a quick, but attentive reading, from beginning to end. Then with a total impression fresh in your mind, divide the manuscript into at least three and not more than seven parts. Draw lines across the page at the boundaries between these major sections.

When you divide the draft into its major sections, ignore typographical and physical divisions in the draft. Don't be afraid to cut a paragraph, or even a long, complicated sentence, in half. After you have drawn the lines, perhaps changed your mind a time or two, and finally decided where each break should occur, take a scissors or straightedge and cut or tear the first draft into its major sections.

The problem now is to devise a temporary system for keeping the major sections separated. You can file each section in an individual Manila folder. Or you can simply tape each section into a long strip and hang it on the wall. Usually the latter method is better, since it makes it easier to see each section as a total unit and since it may encourage you to peck away at the draft whenever there is a spare moment. There is something rather fascinating about a manuscript hanging on a wall in long strips; it is rather like a "wet paint" sign or a partially completed jigsaw puzzle, which insists upon investigation and attention.

But whatever technique you use, the point is to get each major section physically separated, for a time, from the others. When you isolate each section you can better expose the special virtues and problems of each. The procedure is rather like pulling a pearl from a string and isolating it on a piece of velvet, when preparing to restring it or perhaps to give it an entirely new setting.

Minor Sections and Minor Themes

The next step is to divide each major section into at least two but no more than five parts. (If a section persists in having more than five parts, you probably have enough material for another major section. Look very hard at how the material is grouped before you break the rule and admit more than five parts.) As before, read attentively but quickly and draw lines—but do not cut up the manuscript. Most of these parts are minor sections, but some of them may be summary sections that represent major themes. Deciding which are which can best be done after the next step is finished.

Number the minor sections. A highlighter felt pen is good for this job. Now number an equal quantity of blank sheets of paper, one sheet for each minor section. Read each section, then summarize it in one sentence on its numbered sheet. Keep trying. Use up the entire sheet. Get at least ten to twelve different sentences, each of which tries to summarize its section neatly, freshly, compactly. These summary sentences are statements of your minor themes.

SUMMARY SENTENCES: TOPICS AND COMMENTS

It is sound economy to spend as much time as you need to get good summary sentences. To get them, you should use to its fullest each part of the sentence. Use the normal subject-predicate pattern of English, making sure that each part of the sentence refers directly to the important material in the section being summarized. First you should tell your reader what it is you are talking about—that is, what the *topic* of the section is. Then you should tell him what you are saying about your topic—that is, what the section's *comment* is.

If the topic of the section is dead fish, make that topic the subject of your summary sentence. Then determine what your comment is, what you are saying about dead fish, and use that as the predicate of your sentence. A good summary sentence might be something like this: "Dead fish smell bad, get slimy, and attract flies."

Avoid the temptation to use abstraction or generalization rather than condensation to create a summary sentence. This temptation is a serious one, because loose generalization and abstraction are easier than is accurate condensation. A summary should stay at exactly the same level of abstraction and the same degree of generalization as the material it is summarizing. A good summary sentence is like condensed soup: You take out the air and water, but leave in the meat and vegetables. The flavor should remain in the summary—if anything, it should be even stronger because of the condensation.

Again, don't settle for your first, easy try. You want an honest meaty summary sentence. Don't settle for a sentence such as, "This section is about dead fish," since this kind of sentence has only two words in it that pertain to the topic and none that refer to the com-

Identifying and Naming Topics

ment. A good summary sentence must include a subject and a predicate that correspond to the topic and comment of the section.

In a given section of expository or descriptive prose it is usually easy to identify the topic. In expository and descriptive prose, the topic of a passage often is also the grammatical subject of the sentences that make up the passage:

> He was extraordinarily crude and ill-mannered. He wiped his nose on his fingers, his fingers on his shirt. He preferred shouting to talking, and if he could do neither, he pouted and grew surly.

Whoever the lout is, he is the topic of the passage and the persistent topic and subject of each sentence. Gossip in all its forms, literary or conversational, is marked by passages of this kind.

The topic of a passage is not always specified by its grammatical subjects, however, as can be seen if the foregoing description were continued:

> He was extraordinarily crude and ill-mannered. He wiped his nose on his fingers, his fingers on his shirt. He preferred shouting to talking, and if he could do neither, he pouted and grew surly. His face would get shiny as he shouted, but turn a dull greasy pink when sullen. His hair curled around small ears. Each ear had, for its size, a remarkably long lobe.

Even when those three sentences are added to the description of the lout, and when the resulting passage is analyzed as a single unit, the lout remains the topic of the passage—and of each sentence—even though he ceases to be the subject of the last three sentences.

Of course, if any of those last three sentences were analyzed alone and out of context, confusion would set in; for each then would have to be interpreted as having a different topic. In isolation the topics would be first "face," then "hair," then "ears." It is because of semantic tricks such as these that early editorial work should concentrate on entire passages and not on isolated sentences.

That a topic or a comment is recurring may be momentarily obscured if a variety of words have been used to name the same idea.

Synonyms have their place, but not in summary sentences. With the sentences in front of you, check carefully for recurrent topics or comments lurking behind a façade of vocabulary that is too wide for the job at hand. The unifying ideas in your paper need to be found, and each of them should be given a precise and fitting name—either a single word or a very short phrase. The ideal name is short enough to be repeated without clanking too much on the ear, since the names of key concepts are likely to be repeated. But most important, the ideal name highlights with precision and clarity the topic or the comment in question.

As you set out naming, you almost always will find that you have more terms of recurrent concepts than you really need. Underneath a variety of terms you often begin to notice synonyms or near synonyms that indicate a common reference or perhaps a common attitude. In such a situation your job simply will be to find that single word or short phrase that pinpoints exactly the common, underlying idea. Sometimes the word or phrase already will be there in your draft; sometimes you will have to search for a new one.

Sometimes, rather than having more names than you need, you will discover that a key term you have used repeatedly, far from being well defined, actually covers disparities and differences that deserve names of their own. In either case, if you have trouble finding the name you need, turn to your dictionary. Look closely at the definitions of the terms involved. Look, too, at the synonymy studies in your desk dictionary or, if you have one, in your dictionary of synonyms. Look, finally, at the etymologies of crucial terms, to try to get some sense of the word's ancestry. You may even find a thesaurus helpful here, but remember how a thesaurus should be used. (See pages 44–46 for a discussion of dictionaries and thesauri.)

Problems With Narrative Summaries

Summarizing narrative passages is more complex than summarizing expository passages. The topic of a narrative passage is the main *agent*—that is, the person or thing acting in the passage. The comment is the agent's *action*:

> Dr. Nyet touched the button. Kitty tensed. The mechanism began to hum slightly. A metal arm moved back, then over. The record

dropped and the strains of the "Third Man Theme" filled the room.

The narrative topic, or agent, in this passage is Dr. Nyet. The comment, or action, is the seduction of Kitty. So the summary of the action—or the *synopsis*—would be: "Dr. Nyet seduces Kitty." But the narratives you will most often be writing in college will be exempla—narratives with a moral, narratives that have a general meaning beyond the specific acts described.

A complete summary of a passage of such narrative involves not only a synopsis but also an explicit statement of the general meaning of the passage. As was pointed out earlier (see pp. 88–91), sometimes you want to spell out explicitly for your reader the meanings of such exempla; sometimes you want to leave them implicit. But always you will want to make an explicit statement for yourself as part of the job of gaining editorial control over your material.

The general meaning of an exemplum depends not only on the exemplum itself but also on the rhetorical uses you are putting it to in your paper. Thus, in a paper that was analyzing Kitty's character the meaning of the scene with her and Dr. Nyet might be: "Her seduction brings to the surface Kitty's sexual abandon and marks the beginning of her moral decay." But in a paper that was analyzing Dr. Nyet the meaning might be: "Though mad and evil, Dr. Nyet is sensitive to the finer things." The same exemplum can serve more than one generality. Otherwise the events of the reign of Henry VIII would only have been told one way.

Notice, then, these three things about narrative passages: (1) They need two summaries—a synopsis of the action and a statement of its more general meaning. (2) The statement of meaning depends on the use to which you plan to put the passage in your paper. (3) The statement of meaning, unlike the synopsis, will be more abstract and general than the action within the passage itself.

The Naked "This"

In a rough draft one of the most common symptoms of the need to name a topic explicitly is the naked "this." The naked "this" is very common in first drafts, especially in reports that involve the narration of events. After many pages of closely written narrative that detail a series of actions, which, say, culminated in the defeat of bloody Harry Morgan on the high seas, a student may move on to a new section with a statement such as, "This caused the British Empire to appoint . . ." This what? The writer is not simply referring back to the idea or the action of the previous sentence, a use of "this" that is acceptable enough most of the time; but rather he is using "this" to cover all that happened in the preceding pages. The use of a naked "this" in such circumstances will be at best vague, at worst misleading and confusing.

Because each large episode inevitably is described as a series of smaller actions, war historians long ago learned to give definite names to large, complex episodes, to better handle the problem of generalizing about them: "The Battle of Bull Run," "Custer's Last Stand," "Cornpone's Disaster." If you want to make a generalization about the effects of a series of actions, you need a handy, brief way of referring to the entire series. The method is simple enough. Give a name to the whole episode, taking care to mark its bounds:

> The Battle of the Ransomed Daughters began when Harry Morgan offered his services to Drake's grandson. The offer involved the transfer of one thousand slaves, the razing of Saint Augustine, and the ransom of three unmarried daughters of the Spanish viceroy. It ended with the city untouched, the daughters dead, and Morgan's ships scattered from the mouth of the Amazon to the banks of North Carolina.

Once you have marked the boundaries of an episode and have christened it (if it doesn't already have a name, invent one), then later you will be able to say unambiguously, "The Battle of the Ransomed Daughters caused the British Parliament to . . ." The name need not be dramatic, but it must be explicit.

The tactic of naming should not be limited to war histories; it works for other subjects, too. "The Great Portage of the Vikings," "The Strike at Holmes Dining Hall," "The Erosion of the American Dollar," "The Enlightened Actions of the New College Coed"—whatever the title, whatever the subject, its boundaries can be marked and named. It should be named early enough in the draft to clothe each and every naked "this."

The somewhat elaborate procedure discussed in this section might seem like quite a fuss to make over so simple a thing as a name, but finding exactly the right name is very important. A name is more than a label; it is a way to take something that is outside you and put it into your mind. A name is a way to control something. Remember that Adam's first job in Eden, after he was given dominion over the animals, was to sit down and give every one of them a name. If you want to gain dominion over your draft material, take the time to find the right name for your key concepts.

The Major Themes

Choose among the attempts the one sentence that best summarizes each minor section. (It is apt to be a composite sentence made up of bits and pieces of different attempts.) On a blank sheet of paper list these, your best attempts at stating your minor themes. List them according to the tentative sequence you have decided upon for your first draft—allowing, of course, for any promising changes you may have made since then. Mark off the major sections on the list; then summarize each of them. Suppose, for instance, that the first three minor sections constitute your first major section. You now can ponder summary sentences one, two, and three, and then summarize their contents in one juicy sentence. Do the same for each of the other major sections. Again, give yourself several tries. And, again, choose your best efforts as the official statements of the major themes.

Sometimes the job is easy. One of the summary sentences in a group may already be a summary of the entire group. This situation may occur whenever you have sections that recapitulate other sections. Other times the job is not so easy, and you may have to use every syntactic trick you know to get everything into that one sentence. For example, below is a group of summary sentences that a student decided was representative of one major section of her paper on insurance:

1. Generally, people know little about the important factors in purchasing insurance.
2. Life insurance is probably the insurance most misused.
3. Most ordinary car insurance needs are covered by five basic types of car insurance, here listed in order of importance: liability, comprehensive, collision, medical payments, and uninsured motorist.

4. Health insurance covering five areas is available from several sources with either cash or service benefits.

The student's next job was to summarize all of that into one sentence. Of the various summaries that were attempted this one seemed to be the best. For one thing, its parallel clauses strongly suggest a better organization of the material than the one used for the first draft and reflected in the list of minor themes.

> People who buy insurance usually don't know enough about health insurance to shop comparatively; they know less about car insurance, for they often slight the most important coverages; they know least of all about life insurance, for most people buy the wrong kind, for the most money.

This final edited statement of a major theme showed up some weaknesses in the initial list of minor themes, since the student had to draw upon material she knew but had not summarized as yet to get the major summary sentence done properly. She then went back and rewrote the summary sentences on health and car insurance to get the "moral" of the sections into her summary—that is, the points about the lack of comparative shopping and about the slighting of priorities. Checking back to her draft, she found that the moral lay in her material ready to be highlighted, but had so far been neglected.

The Master Theme

After drafting summary sentences that state your minor and major themes, it remains only to draft a summary sentence that summarizes your entire manuscript—that is, a statement of its "master theme." Of all the summary sentences, this one—not too surprisingly—is usually the most difficult to write, primarily because it condenses more material than you have condensed before. But a sharp and forceful statement of the master theme is worth considerable effort, for sometimes, if pushed hard enough, your mind can find just the right combination, and out will come a sentence that puts the cap on the whole manuscript. A good statement of your master theme can provide one of those climactic sentences that snaps the sections into place, tightens the entire draft, and leaves the argument and intent clearly in view, pulling pieces together with a new tautness. Here is such a statement of the master theme from a student's paper on heart transplants:

> A doctor can pronounce me dead, take my heart and transplant it in another person, but he cannot technically or ethically justify the procedure by saying that my heart was more useful in the recipient than it would have been left in me.

A statement of master theme as good as this does much to help pinpoint and guide the final editorial tightening that remains. This particular one helped highlight a basic theme that ran through the student's zero and first drafts but that somehow had not become visible before. With a few more touches and some patches and cuts, that theme helped bring all of what she had to say together—once she saw that it was there.

It is worthwhile to spend considerable time trying for a good statement of your master theme. If you should dig into the job only to come to doubt that you will ever find the right combination of lucky words—or the lucky combination of right words—don't be afraid to ask for help. Ask someone—a professor perhaps, or simply a friend—to read your draft and tell you what he thinks you've said.

Admittedly, most statements of your master themes will be too thick, too lumpy, and just too much to be easily used in your final draft. They usually have to be broken up and distributed a bit.

Even if you never use a direct statement of the master theme in your final draft, drafting one makes you more aware of exactly what it is you are trying to say to a reader. Determining the recurrent topics and comments in a draft, dividing it into major and minor sections, writing the summary sentences that state explicitly the themes—the goal of all these basic editorial procedures is to make you more aware of what you have said and what you must say to a reader.

This awareness is extremely important, for it is the basic guide for editorial decisions. Such decisions are made not on the basis of some quest for qualities such as unity, emphasis, and coherence, viewed in the abstract. The editorial decisions that either do or do not produce these qualities are always made in terms of specific contexts. Questions of unity depend on an awareness of what you are trying to say to your reader. Questions of coherence depend on your sense of how much he knows about what you are trying to say. Questions of emphasis depend on your sense of what he needs to be told at this time.

10 EDITING THE FIRST DRAFT: THE SENTENCE OUTLINE

Once you have the summary sentences prepared, it would be a good idea to gather together those sentences that provide the best statements of your master, major, and minor themes into a sentence outline. A sentence outline is usually not too useful before drafting, because the only honest sentence outline is one that condenses material that is already written. In a curious way most students discover this on their own, usually while still in high school. When told by a teacher to write a sentence outline first, then to write the paper, then to turn in the outline and the paper, most students almost invariably write the paper before the outline. Thousands of students seem to have learned inadvertently—though they have not always taken advantage of it—one of the major lessons of writing: *There can't be a good summary sentence until there is something written to summarize.*

An honest sentence outline can serve a number of different purposes. When editing first draft into more finished form, a sentence outline can show just what has been said, disclosing gaps and weaknesses as well as strengths. Neatly typed and presented with the manuscript, the sentence outline can offer a set of promises to the editor or teacher who must evaluate the manuscript. Perhaps an even better time to show an instructor a sentence outline would be *before* the final paper is turned in to be judged. The instructor's reactions can be of great value, if you have given yourself enough time to incorporate any changes that he might suggest. Meanwhile, the list of summary sentences that comprise the outline serves as a scale model of your manuscript. Diagnosing it will, in effect, be diagnosing your entire draft.

Because a good summary sentence names the topic of its section in the subject and the comment in the predicate, a list of such sentences quickly reveals the basic rhetorical pattern of the first draft. There are only a few basic patterns; the three most common are described below.

Pattern 1. The topic stays the same, but the comment varies:

Guns	hurt people.
Guns	are bought too easily.
Guns	should be harder to get.

Because this pattern repeats the topic, it has the advantage of inevitably producing a sense of unity; and because it varies the comment, even the most random variation will smell vaguely logical, whereas, at its most formal, it is probably a tight and proper logical argument. Either way, the pattern tends to be persuasive. It does have some disadvantages: In descriptive writing the pattern is very natural and common, but it can produce the mechanical formality of a second-rate encyclopedia if it is not somehow varied from time to time. In argumentative writing that pounds on a single topic, as in Pattern 1, you must take care to avoid the more infamous logical fallacies.

Pattern 2. The topic varies, but the comment remains the same:

The administration	is corrupt and should be abolished.
The military	is corrupt and should be abolished.
The church	is corrupt and should be abolished.
Society	is corrupt and should be abolished.

This pattern has some definite advantages: For one thing, it is fairly easy to write; for another, because the comment is repeated, the pattern inevitably produces a consistency of stance and basic tone. Its main disadvantage is that it could begin to bore the reader because he soon will learn that he can predict the comment. At least in longer papers, most readers demand a comment that is less predictable. Readers expect the comment to be new information; one fairly easy way to satisfy those readers would be to switch Pattern 2 into Pattern 1 by converting the comment into the topic, and vice versa. Remember, though, that this switch sometimes requires agile writing to keep short verbs and short adjectives from turning into long nouns. For example, switching the topic and comment of the first sentence in the list above so that it fits the form of Pattern 1 could easily lead to a horror such as, "Corruption and the need for abolition typify the administration," when probably what is needed is a longer sentence with shorter words, such as "One thing that is corrupt and needs to be abolished is the administration." (Remember, too, that rewriting a summary sentence in this way probably means recasting somewhat the section it summarizes.)

Pattern 3. Topics and comments both vary, with comments becoming the next topic:

People who eat large quantities of fried chicken	neglect to eat chicken broth.
Chicken broth	is a nourishing national resource.
This nourishing national resource	is getting scarce.
This scarcity	is aggravated when certain Kentucky colonels proliferate fried chicken stands.

Pattern 3 has two main advantages: First, it makes the transition problems from section to section minimal; second, it provides the constant, though controlled, variation that can counter the monotony built into Pattern 2 and hovering in the background of Pattern 1. The main disadvantage of this pattern is that each point of transition can turn one of several directions, so that the writing can quickly begin to wander, meandering from point to point like an endless, shaggy-dog story. The chain produced in Pattern 3 must be made to circle back somehow, for if it does not return at the end to some earlier topic or comment, the effect can be as if a long chain were arbitrarily cut to a length convenient for the writer. The required circle can encompass some or all of the essay, but usually the best tactic is to close the chain where it can best circle back to the opening, as the preceding example returns to chicken broth and fried chicken.

The three basic patterns can be mixed one with the other; but there does not appear to be enough standardization of the ways that they can be mixed to warrant much description here. The rule of thumb to follow amidst the variety of possible patterns is to try to gain a satisfactory sense of form. The reason for making and diagnosing a sentence outline is to get some sense of organization. Though not a guarantee of it, organization is a first step toward this sense of form.

11 HOW TO CREATE A SENSE OF FORM

Organization is having each thing in its place. The insides of a desk drawer are organized if the person using the desk knows what goes where in it. The scheme by which things get organized, however, can be thoroughly arbitrary and nonrational: There is nothing logical about the order of the alphabet, for example, yet it can be used to organize an entire library. To someone unfamiliar with the alphabetical scheme, a library might appear to be a disordered array of tall books next to short ones, thick ones shouldering thin ones, blue ones clashing against green ones. So, too, is it with a paper. A paper may be well organized without having form. The order of its parts may be a triumph of logical analysis, and the writer may be in full control of what parts go where and why. He can be fully aware that his argument goes from point A through point D to point F, but unless the reader is also aware of this, there will not be a sense of form. With his work in front of him and his outline neatly finished, a writer can know what to expect, so he can see "form" where a reader who does not know what to expect can see none.

As Kenneth Burke's famous definition puts it:

> Form is the creation of an appetite in the mind of the auditor, and the adequate satis-

fying of that appetite. This satisfaction—so complicated is the human mechanism—at times involves a temporary set of frustrations, but in the end these frustrations prove to be simply a more involved kind of satisfaction, and furthermore serve to make the satisfaction of fulfillment more intense.[1]

The reader is led to expect something, perhaps is teased a bit, and then his expectations are fulfilled. He is encouraged to look for something and his hope is gratified. The form a paper has is the form the writer prepares his reader to see. Form is something a reader sees when promises made to him are kept.

Thus, a sentence outline, seen only by an author and his editor, cannot help the reader one whit. Before it can help the reader get a sense of form, the outline must be absorbed into the paper and used to set up the reader's expectations. As long as the summary sentences remain in the outline only, they do not help a reader see form. The reader must be given the promises that an outline incorporates. Every one of those summary sentences should be put to good use in the paper itself in a way that will give a reader a sense of promises fulfilled.

PROMISES AND FORM

Obviously, summary sentences are useful within the sections they summarize, where they can operate as topic or thesis sentences. But summary sentences have uses beyond the section they summarize. They are the most powerful of the cues and links available to a writer for binding together his material so as to give a reader a persuasive sense of form. In some papers the opening paragraph can successfully use six or eight summary sentences as early promises. A paragraph may start with a sentence that summarizes the previous four and a half paragraphs and may end with a sentence that summarizes (in a promissory way) what is forthcoming in the next six paragraphs. In some papers a paragraph or two toward the end can use half the material in the sentence outline in an effective recapitulation.

If the overall organization is of a progressive or syllogistic kind, then summary sentences can work within their own domains and afterward can work as reminders to the reader of what has been said.

If the material has no built-in progression of its own, then summary sentences may be needed ahead of the section they summarize to set up the expectations that, when satisfied, will give the material form.

A writer can make three otherwise diverse and separate sections cohere in a reader's mind if, at the start, the reader is warned and is ready for them. A reader does not start out questioning an author; he does not start out asking, "Why?" But he might ask that question later—if he comes to things he does not expect. In a paper covering three radically different topics, if a reader is not told what to expect until the point of transition, needless problems can be created for him. Neither tinkering at the transition points nor relying on "howevers" or "moreovers" will work as well as simply telling a reader what to expect early enough for him to accept it. An early promise can forestall major transitional problems before a reader gets to them. A reader must know what to expect if he is to get a satisfactory sense of form.

Sometimes a student-writer will work hard to get good summary sentences and then plant them in a draft to set up or reaffirm a reader's expectations, only to become painfully aware of how "artificial" the sentences are. Specifically crafted and put into the "natural" prose, these sentences may seem to be latecoming intruders, but one of the beauties of writing is that no one needs to know where or what the latecomers are. Retyping should wipe away all traces of late patching, so that everything that fits will look "natural." The summary sentences should no longer look out of place; they just might seem that way to a student-writer who is a novice and is very conscious of how they were deliberately crafted to set up expectations.

Don't be misled by the simplicity of the devices. At the start of a paper it is the writer's game. A reader will accept the rules—if he is told what they are. He will accept as a promissory note that he is going to read an essay about cabbages, firecrackers, and menthol cigarettes. If the writer fulfills those promises in the essay, the reader's expectation will be satisfied, however minimal that satisfaction might be. He will discern form.

HOW TO USE PRO-FORMS

Abbreviated clues that set up expectations can be called "pro-forms," because they do what pronouns do. Just as a pronoun can refer to and substitute for another—usually longer—word or phrase or sentence, so pro-forms represent other, longer sections of prose. A pro-form can be a single word, a single phrase, or a full summary sentence. Each can represent a minor section, a major section, or the whole of a work. Thus, both the size of the hint and the amount it promises can vary.

When a reader is promised a section on a specific topic, he doesn't have to be told everything that is to follow. Sometimes promises should be explicit; then a full summary sentence is necessary. But often only a hint of what is to come is needed, so that just the names of the major topics will be enough.

Pro-forms have three basic positions: (1) as part of the section they abbreviate, (2) before the section they abbreviate, and (3) after the section they abbreviate. Put ahead of the section they abbreviate, they act as coy hints or full promises, depending upon whether they are single words or fully explicit summary sentences. Placed after the section, they act as reminders, quietly alluding to or fully recapitulating the section they represent.

To illustrate how this works, we will examine a section from the middle of a paper and list the pro-forms for the comment it makes. Then we will decide what help they might be in editing the section. Later we will see how pro-forms can be used outside the section they represent. Following is a section from a first draft of a theme titled "The Aesthetic Function of Language." The paragraph starts out with a sentence that alludes back and summarizes the opening sections of the paper. The second sentence prepares the way for new material, so that the section to be abbreviated actually starts with the third sentence of the paragraph:

> It was as a small boy in those quiet places that I learned about the artificiality and the reality of words. It was, of course, a lesson learned outside of school. *In school I had to memorize long poems—poems about Thanksgiving, about Christmas, even Ground-hog's Day and basketball victories. Later—again in private—I learned that poetry is only indirectly and casually about subjects like the Fourth of July or romantic love or Lincoln's birthday. Whatever else it is about, poetry always is a celebration of the act of language.*

Poetry is clearly the topic of the section; the comment is something about celebrating. The tentative, short pro-forms, then, are (1) "poetry" and (2) "celebrate," and its various forms—"celebrates," "celebrating," "celebration," "celebrants."

Once it is clear that the comment is about celebrations, then in the first rewrite that idea should be included as soon as possible and as often as possible, just to see what can be done:

> In my schools, I was made to memorize poems that celebrated Thanksgiving and Christmas, that celebrated Ground-hog's Day and basketball victories. It was only later, much later, and again in private, that I learned that poetry only inadvertently and in a transient sort of way celebrates events like the Fourth of July or a marriage, romantic love or Lincoln's birthday. What poetry always is, is a celebration of the act of language itself.

The use of the verb "celebrates," rather than the noun "celebration," is effective enough to suggest that the final sentence should be revised: "The event that poetry always celebrates is the act of language itself." However, now there are too many "celebrations" in a very short number of lines. The final version might go like this:

> It was as a boy in those quiet places that I learned about the artificiality and the reality of words. It was, of course, a lesson learned outside of school. *In my schools, I memorized poems to celebrate Thanksgiving, Christmas, Ground-hog's Day, Parent's Day, even basketball victories. It was only later, much later, and again in private, that I learned that poetry only inadvertently and in a transient sort of way celebrates events like the Fourth of July or a marriage, romantic love or Lincoln's birthday. The event that poetry always and permanently celebrates is the act of language itself.*

Within the section itself judicious use of one of the pro-forms can prepare the reader for the final statement at the end, thereby encouraging a sense of form.

A sense of form may be especially important if sections do not cohere inevitably, one to another. When faced with sections that lack coherence, a writer may need the formal aid that the promises of pro-forms can provide. The terms "coherence" and "incoherence" are used in a special way here. Whereas "incoherence" is used most often to refer to words that don't make sense, something different, something more precise is meant here. And since the decision about where to use and how to use pro-forms depends upon the degree of coherence that one's material contains, let us examine more closely a more precise definition of coherence.

NOTE

1. Kenneth Burke, "Psychology and Form," *Counter-Statement,* 2d ed. (Los Altos, Calif.: Hermes, 1953), p. 31.

12 SEQUENCE, COHERENCE, AND TRANSITION

We define "coherence" simply as a fixed sequence. A three-part paper is coherent if the first part must come before the second part, and if the second part must come before the third. If each part makes enough sense alone that there is no fixed sequence, the sections do not cohere. Things cohere when, like the parts of a jigsaw puzzle, they have only one place in which they fit. Parts cohere if they presuppose other parts.

We have already seen that coherence is not the same thing as "form," nor is it the same as "unity," for as we shall see shortly, a paper can have unity and still lack coherence. Coherence also is not the same as "organization," for even a precise scheme of classification does not guarantee coherence. Suppose a student has set up very precise definitions and has used them to sort out Socialists from Democrats, Democrats from Republicans, and Republicans from reactionaries. This would be the kind of organization that could be outlined:

1. Socialists differ from Democrats in that . . .
2. Democrats differ from Republicans in that . . .
3. Republicans differ from reactionaries in that . . .

If the definitions are adequate, a paper based upon such a scheme will be well organized—yet as long as no part of the discussion presupposes any other part of the discussion, there will be no special coherence in such a scheme, no sense of a fixed and necessary sequence.

The determination of what presupposes what depends upon how much a writer thinks his reader knows. Perhaps you have heard bad joke-tellers, who get to the punch line only to remember a crucial detail that was left out: "Oh, I forgot, first I should have told you, the fellow was a traveling salesman, see, and he was broke. . . ." With that bit of information the joke is still badly told, but at least the punch line can make sense. Many stories and essays depend on the reader knowing certain things before the climactic section. Some papers lack coherence simply because their authors forget to put in things their readers need to know at the time they need to know them.

To decide that a certain part of a paper may be impossible, or at least difficult, to understand unless other parts appear first is to make a decision about coherence. Decisions about coherence, then, are based upon assumptions about the reader. Suppose you have written a passage about sheepherding; to understand that passage a reader first must know something about sheep dogs. If you assume he knows about sheep dogs, you say nothing about them, except through an allusion or two, perhaps. If you assume that he does not know about sheep dogs, then you must write another passage that will tell him what he needs to know. And the passage dealing with sheep dogs must come before the one dealing with sheepherding.

Though students sometimes imagine that the way the parts come out of the typewriter the first time is inviolable, actually very few essays have major and minor sections that have fixed and immutable sequences. Coherence is not very common. It does not come in large hunks; it comes in strands of varied length and power. Unless one is writing a set of mathematical demonstrations, it is unlikely that a draft will have many long, powerful strands of coherence.

Most material contains only a few of these valuable strands. For example, the paper that sorted Socialists from Democrats and went on to define other political types might easily have contained a strand. Suppose the student discovered that to make the distinction between Socialists and Democrats clear he had to use a new, relatively unknown definition of capitalism. Obviously the definition had to come before the passage that made the distinction between the two parties. It may have been a short strand of coherence, but it was a real one, nevertheless.

Strands may bind paragraphs within a section, one minor section to another, or major sections that, within themselves, may be rather incoherent. For example, a paper on Che Guevara might have as its master theme the proposition that the guerilla leader's success in Cuba foreshadowed his failure in Bolivia or, conversely, that his failure darkly mirrored his success. If the writer assumes that the reader knows little of the reasons for the success in Cuba, it necessarily will have two sections: one describing the success and one describing the failure. As soon as the theme is stated, the one section immediately will presuppose the other. Each of these major sections, however, then may be composed of minor sections that do not demand a special sequence—for instance, sections dealing with such topics as logistics, recruitment, native support. In such cases the form within each major section is that of a simple list, a string of beads that can be restrung any number of different ways. We will return to this example again later to see how a simple list can be given a more complex form and how it can be provided with linking transitions to give it a sense of coherence.

HOW TO HANDLE SEMI-COHERENT AND INCOHERENT DRAFT

In itself, a first draft that is not coherent is neither good nor bad; it is just a fact that has to be faced, like being six feet nine inches tall or having freckles. It does mean that the author has a different editorial problem than he would have if the parts did cohere. In a way, lack of coherence implies more editorial freedom. The material is more mobile.

When judging the degree of coherence among the parts of a draft, an author is faced with one of three basic situations: *total coherence,* in which the major sections and the minor sections within each section cohere, a highly unlikely situation except in such things as mathematical drafts; *semi-coherence,* in which there is a strand or two of coherence linking major sections or some of the minor sections, a much more common situation; *incoherence,* in which neither major nor minor sections cohere, also a very common situation. Total coherence is so uncommon that we shall let it pass by with no further comment.

It is not at all unusual to have a paper unified around a certain field, with each of the main themes worthy of attention, but with none of them cohering in any obvious or useful way. One part does not explain the other part, and either part could come first as far as the reader is concerned. Often the main themes of such papers are unified insofar as they all make comments about the same general topic (as in Pattern 1 described in Chapter 10), but some papers are more tenuously unified and rely solely on persistent attitudes and tones. A travelogue, for instance, will often contain sections that are within the same essay only because of the nature of the assignment—first Rome, then Istanbul, then New Delhi, for example. The only unity such an essay has is one of tones and perhaps implied comments. The timetable of the trip does not necessarily fix an order to the parts, for the story does not have to start at the beginning of the trip and end with the unpacking of the suitcase. Chronology is not coherence.

The survey article is a common form of writing that groups together miscellaneous items according to some arbitrary criterion like chronology (such as "Nineteenth-Century Poetry"), or geography (such as "American Poetry"), or both (such as "Eighteenth-Century British Poetry").

When a writer starts plotting for form, he must decide how much coherence his material actually has. Then he must decide how much form he wants his reader to discern. Sometimes the various parts do not cohere and do not need to. Sometimes a writer may even want to emphasize a lack of coherence; but even then he must warn his reader not to expect any. He might call the essay "Random Thoughts" or put dates on the various sections and pretend they are entries in a journal, or he might state the situation straightforwardly, as John Colombo does: "I am numbering my points, not because it is fashionable to do so today *à la* Susan Sontag, but because the points are unrelated and taken at random." [1]

On the Use of Numbers

Because everyone knows that number three comes after number two, numbering can give a thin veneer of form to incoherent lists. It is a popular device in rotogravure sections of Sunday papers, such as in articles titled "The Seven Keys to Successful Friendship," and it is also popular among authors of education texts, as seen in titles such as "The Five Factors that Stimulate Good Interpersonal Relationships." Of course, numbers alone are not much of a promise to the reader, since they tell little of what the contents are to be. For the most part they help the reader keep track of how much more there is to endure. Do you remember that inward groan you felt the last time you heard a speaker say, "And now, my seventh point is . . . ." when you knew he had five more dreary points to go? Numbers are fine—up to about seven—but they are hardly sufficient as promises. When aiming for something more than a thin veneer of form, you need promises that tell something of what is to come. You need, in short, those pro-forms discussed in the previous chapter, those abbreviated representatives of entire sections of your paper.

Using Early Promises to Fix a Sequence

The use of promises can lend a sense of coherence to a basically incoherent paper. For instance, if you not only promise to discuss cabbages, firecrackers, and menthol cigarettes, but also imply or state directly that you are going to *first* talk about cabbages, *then* about firecrackers, and *finally* about menthol cigarettes, your promises include a fixed sequence for your discussion. Perhaps it is a sequence as arbitrary as the alphabet, but it *is* fixed. Even so slight a device can add something like a touch of coherence to a paper.

One student, who drafted copiously and actively, had to concede, as he moved to the editing phase, that his material fell into four clear, but quite separate, parts. The parts were all about baseball, so there was simple unity to his work, but there was no connection among the parts that demanded any special sequence. Since, he thought, each would be equally interesting to the reader he had in mind, there was no compelling reason to put one before another. Each part was interesting, each was well written; they simply did not cohere. The student was worried, since he wanted the effect of one, single paper, not four separate ones. The editorial solution was fairly easy and is the standard solution for handling basically incoherent parts when simple clarity is the prime goal: He used summary sentences and other pro-forms early in the paper as promises to the reader.

The final version of the baseball paper successfully employed five summary sentences, which were taken from the sentence outline, in the first paragraph. The reader was promised four distinct, but separate, problems in a given sequence. The promise was fulfilled; a minimal but adequate sense of coherence was assured. The student used a sentence or two to state the master theme and several sentences stating the main themes, which provided early and explicit promises—the prime concern when parts do not cohere.

> As spring approaches, baseball managers start worrying overtime. If nothing else has come up, they can always start by worrying about franchise problems. About the time they get that one settled, they can begin to worry about holdouts. Then come the bonus babies. Finally they can get around to worrying about injuries to key players, a worry guaranteed to keep them busy until the bitter end of the season.

(It is worth mentioning, perhaps, that the paper ended with a brief recapitulation to remind the reader that all of the promises had been kept.)

Turning an Outline Inside Out

Very often the major sections of a paper cohere, but the minor sections do not. The paper on Che Guevara mentioned earlier had a master theme that linked two major sections coherently: "Guevara failed in Bolivia for the same reasons that he succeeded in Cuba." Whether the student started with the section on Bolivia or the section on Cuba, once the master theme was stated and once a section was begun, the second section was immediately implied and anticipated.

The student's first organization of the material fell into a pattern typical for comparisons, a pattern that keeps the two areas of comparison apart. The student's first topic outline was:

I. Reasons for success in Cuba
   A. Logistics
   B. Landownership
   C. Recruitment
   D. Tactics

II. Reasons for failure in Bolivia
   A. Logistics

B. Landownership
C. Recruitment
D. Tactics

Notice that the single strand of coherence links the two major sections, while within each major section there are no special strands of coherence linking any of the minor sections. The points of comparison in each major section are arranged in a simple list, with no special reason for the sequence of the list.

Probably, the first thing an editor would do would be to turn the outline inside out. There are, by the nature of things, always more minor sections than major sections in a paper. To get a greater sense of coherence when major sections cohere but minor sections do not, turn the organization inside out. Not all papers will turn inside out neatly, but when they do, the strands of coherence can be increased, and thus the total sense of coherence can be increased. When the outline of the Guevara paper is turned inside out, there are four short strands linking minor sections, instead of one strand of coherence linking two major sections.

I. Logistics
   A. Cuba
   B. Bolivia

II. Landownership
   A. Cuba
   B. Bolivia

III. Recruitment
   A. Cuba
   B. Bolivia

IV. Tactics
   A. Cuba
   B. Bolivia

In the first organization there are at least six points of transition that are apt to cause some problems. They lie between adjacent parts that do not cohere. In the "inside out" organization there are only three points of transition that might cause trouble—half as many. Turning the paper inside out still leaves a simple list of major topics: logistics, landownership, recruitment, tactics. Early promises and brief recapitulation are often enough to give such a list a sufficient sense of coherence, as with the baseball paper mentioned earlier.

Making One Topic Dominant

Remember that underneath all the concern with form and coherence lies the old rhetorical problem of persuasion. Form and formality are in themselves persuasive. A printed check complete with signature is more plausible than an I.O.U. scrawled on a matchbook. And a properly engraved twenty dollar bill is more impressive than either. The sheer formality of it persuades. Shape, pattern, order in themselves persuade. If you need the persuasive power of a sense of form that is more complex than that offered by the preceding devices, try making one topic dominant. Again the Guevara paper can serve as an example. The writer needed as much persuasive force as he could get. His single strand of coherence, multiplied repeatedly in the minor sections, was not in itself powerful enough to carry much force. He therefore took his incoherent list of topics and made one of them dominant. He changed a pattern that was like a row of identical beads:

0–0–0–0

into a more complexly articulated pattern of parts ranked under and linked by a dominant part:

```
      0
    ╱   ╲
  0—0—0
```

A more fully articulated pattern is an intrinsically more satisfying form and is therefore more persuasive than a simple list. Of course, to make one topic dominant it is not necessary to turn the parts inside out first. The tactic of making one topic dominant can give any simple list a more complex sense of form.

When you decide to make one topic dominant, choose one that seems, under analysis and with second thoughts, to be more basic than the others, one upon which the other topics can be made to depend. If you can discern no such relationship, then choose a topic that seems most likely to maintain your reader's interest, and make it the dominant topic rhetorically. When drafting to make one topic dominant, begin by stating in a summary, promissory way the relationship that the topic has to each of the other topics. In the Guevara paper the student could discern no basic topic, but he decided that recruitment —which reminded him of draft boards and the United States Army and such things—would be the topic most apt to catch the interest of a college audience. His original opening, "Four major factors contributed to the success . . ." was rewritten as follows:

> A guerilla leader gets recruits the same way the U. S. Army gets theirs: voluntarily and not-so-voluntarily. Unlike the U. S. Army, however, guerilla leaders have been most successful when the recruiting was voluntary. The number of volunteers depends upon who owns the land, the retainment of volunteers depends upon logistics, and the success of the recruits depends upon developing special guerilla tactics.

The student then rewrote the opening of each minor section to tie them in with the problem of recruiting. The section about logistics touched upon recruitment only in passing, but it happened that the matters of landownership and certain aspects of guerilla tactics were more bound up with recruitment than the student first realized. What started as an editorial desire to give a simple list a more complex form became a way of rethinking the material and a source for fresh ideas about the subject.

ON TRANSITIONS

When sections cohere and are in the proper sequence, transitions are not much of a problem. Transitions become a problem when parts do not cohere—and since parts seldom cohere, transitions are a persistent problem for the writer. The solution to the problems of transition starts when the writer decides how much coherence his draft reveals. Parts that cohere usually present the least problem in transition, so, as this chapter has tried to demonstrate, it is wise to get as many adjacent parts as possible linked with strands of coherence.

When the strands are used up, the writer must fall back on the rule to group parts in any way that will minimize transition problems. Until the final typing, the parts of a draft are mobile; they can be moved about to places where parts mesh smoothly.

At this point the unused bits of zero draft may prove useful. (See page 98.) Check them for "leaners"—those sections that jam two or more topics together in too brief a space. These compacted bits of zero draft now might give you a transitional passage—or at least an idea for such a passage.

Finally, a writer can always fall back, for the moment, to simple, explicit promises put early in the paper. And then, if he wishes to ease further the problems at particular points of transition, he ought to review the sections on transitional devices in a good handbook, for he is now beyond the big problems of writing a rough draft.

NOTE

1. John Robert Colombo, "Inside the Trade: An Editor's Notes," *Canadian Literature,* 33 (Summer 1967), 52.

index

abstracts, 25
Altick, Richard, 26
analogies, 76–92
assumptions and implications, 71–72
attributes, 57–65; in analogies, 82–83

backing sheets, 38–40
Barrès, Maurice, 4–5
before-and-after (commonplace), 101–102
beginning to draft, 38–40; de-inhibitors for, 5–16; use of dialogue for, 66–67
Bernstein, Jeremy, 78
bibliography, working, 27–28
biographical sources, 23
bitch-and-pitch (commonplace), 101
blah-blah device, 8
book reviews, 23
brainstorming, 59, 62–64
Bronowski, Jacob, 78–79
Burke, Kenneth, 120–121

card catalogue, 21–22
case history, as exemplum, 87, 88–89
categories, 57–65
Cavanagh, John R., and James B. McGoldrick, 93n
coherence, 126–135
Colombo, John, 129
commonplaces, 100–102
comparison: in analogies, 77–92; and contrast, 102
componential analysis, 56–57, 65n
concepts, 57–58
concrete prose, 47–53

contemplation (meditation), 47–55
Crichton, Robert, 5, 9
crucial attributes of categories, 57–58

definitions as source of analogies, 86–87
de-inhibitors for beginning to draft, 5–16
Descartes, René, 60–61
desk dictionaries, 44–45
dialogue, 66–75
dictionaries, 44–46; as sources of analogies, 85–87; biographical, 23; documentation of material from, 87
direct images, 49–50
documentation, 30–34; of material from dictionaries, 87
drafting. *See* beginning to draft *and* zero draft
dramatic point of view, 50–51
Drucker, Peter, 3, 4

editing process: sorting the zero draft, 97–99; organizing the first draft, 99–103; summarizing the sections of the first draft, 104–115; diagnosing the sentence outline of the first draft, 116–119; creating a sense of form, 120–125; creating a sense of coherence, 126–135
empathy, 53–55
etymological dictionaries, 45–46
etymologies as source of analogies, 85–86
examples, 76–92
exempla, 87–92
expectation and form, 104, 120–124
explicit meanings in exempla, 88–91, 111

fable: as kind of exemplum, 87; traditional, as source of exempla, 91
first draft, 100. *See also* editing process
footnotes and footnoting. *See* documentation
form: and expectation, 104, 120–124; persuasive in itself, 133

Foulke, Adrienne, 16*n*
friends, useful to the writer, 14–15, 115

Ghiselin, Brewster, 11, 13
guides: to periodicals, 21; to sources, 25; Winchell's *Guide to Reference Books,* 24–26
Guitton, Jean, 16*n,* 40

Hemingway, Ernest, 9
hypotheses and questions, 17–18

Idea Machine, 56–65
ideal starter text, 19–26
idiosyncracies, useful to the writer, 15
images: in analogies, 78–79, 85–86; in concrete prose, 47–53
implications and assumptions, 71–72
implicit meanings in exempla, 88–91, 111
incoherence, 128–134
indexes: of book reviews, 23; to periodicals, 21; to source material, 25
inhibitions to drafting, coping with, 5–16
inner-outer (commonplace), 101
International Index, 21

Kant, Immanuel, 56
Koestler, Arthur, 12
Kytle, Ray, 75

"leaners" and transition, 98, 135
logic, a note on, 75
loose-leaf binder system, 37–41

major sections, of first draft, 107
major themes, of first draft, 113–114
master theme, of first draft, 114–115
meditation (contemplation), 47–55
Mencken, H. L., 90
metaphor, as kind of analogy, 78
minor sections, of first draft, 107–108
minor themes, of first draft, 107–108
model, as kind of analogy, 77–78

monologue, converting dialogue into, 74–75

naked "this," 111–113
names, for topics, 109–113
New York Times Index, 21
Nock, Albert J., 89–90
noncrucial attributes of categories, 57–58
notes and notetaking, 26–30
numbers and a sense of coherence, 129–130

omniscient point of view, 50–51
organization, 99–103, 120, 126–127
outlines, 7. *See also* sentence outlines

paper, kinds of, 36–38
parable, as kind of exemplum, 87
periodical guides, 21
personification, as kind of analogy, 81–83
photocopying, and notetaking, 30
place and setup for writing, 13–16
point of view, 50–51
precise prose, 56–65
professors, useful to the writer, 23–24, 115
pro-forms, 122–125
promises and a sense of coherence, 130–131. *See also* expectation and form
prospectus, 6, 18–19

questions and hypotheses, 17–19
quotations in notes, 29–30

range of variation within categories, 72–74
Reader's Guide to Periodical Literature, 21
repetition: when drafting, 8; when editing, 104
revising. *See* editing process
rituals, useful to the writer, 10–16

same-and-different (commonplace), 102
scenes: in contemplation, 47–55; in exempla, 87
schedules for writing, 11–13
sectioning the first draft, 106–108
self-image, important to the writer, 5–6
semi-coherence, 128–134
sensations and images, 49–50
senses, questioning them to describe a scene, 51–53
sentence outlines, 116–119, 121; turning one inside out, 131–133
serendipity, 34–35, 91
setting, for dialogue, 69
setup and place for writing, 13–16
sources, finding and using, 17–35
specimens, 76–77
strips, for drafting, 38
style, for dialogue, 69–70
style manuals, 33–34
summary sentences, 104–115; and coherence, 130–131; and form, 121–123. *See also* sentence outlines; topics; *and* themes
synonym dictionaries, 46

tape recorders: and drafting, 42–44; and examples, 76–77; and notetaking, 27
Tharaud, J., 4–5
themes, of the first draft, 105, 107–108, 113–115
thesauri, 46
time for writing, 11–13
tones, control of, 53–55
tools for the writer, 27, 30, 36–46
topics: and comments, 108–113, 117–119, 123–124; making one dominant, 133–134
transitions, 98, 134–135

unconscious mind and productive thought, 4–5, 11–13, 92

vicarious images, 49–50

voices used in dialogue, 67–69, 74

Watts, Allan, 53
Who's Who, 23
Winchell's *Guide to Reference Books,* 23, 24–26
"winging it," 79–80

working bibliography, 27–28

zero draft, 3–16; notes as, 29; sorting of, 97–99. *See also* beginning to draft
zero zero draft, how to cope with, 102–103

About the Authors

JOHN HERUM is Associate Professor of English at Central Washington State College. A graduate of Carroll College, he has done graduate work at Fordham University, the University of Washington, and The Catholic University of America. He has also written and edited technical material for a number of large organizations.

DONALD WAYNE CUMMINGS is Associate Professor of English and Director of Composition at Central Washington State College. He received his Ph.D. from the University of Washington in 1965. His interest lies in language theory, particularly rhetoric and poetics.